JANE CROWFOOT

HOMESPUN
Vintage

20 TIMELESS KNIT AND CROCHET PROJECTS

COLLINS & BROWN

First published in the United Kingdom in 2013 by
Collins & Brown
10 Southcombe Street
London
W14 0RA

An imprint of Anova Books Company Ltd

Copyright © Collins & Brown 2013
Text and pattern/project copyright © Jane Crowfoot 2013

Photography on pages 56 & 60 Christina Wilson, all other
photography by Holly Jolliffe.

Illustrations by Nicola Heidaripour. Charts by Kuo Kang Chen.

Distributed in the United States and Canada by
Sterling Publishing Co, 387 Park Avenue South, New York,
NY 10016-8810, USA

ISBN 978-1-84340-629-7

A CIP catalogue record for this book is available from the
British Library.

10 9 8 7 6 5 4 3 2 1

Reproduction by Mission Productions Ltd, Hong Kong
Printed and bound by 1010 Printing International Ltd, China

This book can be ordered direct from the publisher at
www.anovabooks.com

For Andy, who continues to dream of an alternative life where he is an over~indulged and spoilt husband.

Contents

Introduction

I have always loved wallpaper, paint, carpets, cushions, pillows as well as all those lovely intricate little things like lampshades, candles and ornaments, which, when placed lovingly and eclectically together, create stunning interiors. As a child I was fascinated by the old-fashioned 1930s style of my grandmother's house and the contrasting style of my dad's bedroom, which he had decorated himself in the 1950s. I loved to snuggle up in my candlewick bedspread in the 1970s and admired the psychedelic orange, mustard and brown wallpapers of the time. In my late teens I worked part-time in a paint and decorating store, and by the time I went to art school in the 1980s I was determined that one day I would design and decorate my own home to reflect my passion for interior design, imagining huge murals on the ceilings of tall hallways and rooms of a mammoth scale covered in artwork and textiles from all over the world.

Although the practicalities and outcomes of my dream have of course changed over the years, my adoration of all things related to interior design are as strong as ever, and I consider myself extremely lucky to live in a world where we have so much choice of amazing design at our fingertips. We can choose from an endless list of influences in every aspect of our lives: we can choose the style in which we dress, we can choose what music to listen to and we can even decide what type of food we wish to eat. Like its fashion counterpart, the interior design market sets seasonal trends and there are an abundance of publications that can show you how to create the current 'look'. We can choose to decorate our houses in a contemporary modernist style or we can decide to be more retro, choosing old and new things that work together. We could choose a feminine style with frills, flowers and lace, or we could opt for a more masculine feel with strong lines and a more subtle colour choice. The decisions are ours and we are all free to make whatever choices we want.

I personally believe that our homes should reflect who we are and what goes on within them. For example, I like antiques and treasure the vintage relics I have been lucky enough to have been left by my grandparents. I love the kids' drawings stuck to the fridge with magnets and the piles of books and magazines that never quite make it back to their place on the shelf. I can live with the trainers, football boots and shoes that amass by the back door, and of course I adore the little arrangements of yarn that invariably sit beside me on the couch! All these things are a personal reflection of my family and me and as such I think they are invaluable (if not a little untidy). Of course, we can all make decisions about how we wish to decorate our homes – we can choose the colour scheme and the style, we can make decisions about what type of soft furnishings to have and what type of flooring would best suit our needs, but if we have the added advantage of knowing how to knit, crochet or sew then we have the ability to create those special extra touches that can help us reflect our own personalities and create unique and stunning interiors.

The crafts of knitting and crochet lend themselves superbly to soft home furnishings. A knitted or crochet fabric is invariably stretchy and hardwearing and both crafts can be used to make the most comfortable and attractive cushions, blankets and throws. Knitting and crochet works fantastically well together, but can be equally as exciting when worked alone. I am really proud to present you with this collection of vintage-inspired knitting and crochet projects for the home. In this book you will find unique designs for cushions, throws and blankets, plus a few other pieces such as a doily and a lampshade braid that I have designed with the home interior in mind. Some of the projects are simple and would take very little time to complete, whereas others are more complicated and will require more of an undertaking. The designs are divided into three stories, but there is nothing to stop you from mixing and matching the projects. With such a wealth of yarn quality and colour choice available to us in our modern world; the design variations can be endless.

Jane Crowfoot

Folk Tales

The first decade of the new millennium has seen a rich mix of styles filtering through the world of interior design. Although many designers are embracing the ethos of minimalism once again, there is also a new emphasis on soft furnishings, with cushions, rugs and textiles making a strong impact on otherwise minimalist interiors. Textiles for the home have become bold and intricate as the craft market especially re-explores the arts and crafts of a bygone age to create a focal point for a room. This design story was inspired by naïve painting and imagery and folkloric heritage. Russian and Scandinavian influences abound. Birds and flowers, bright coloured stripes and beads and pom poms are plentiful. Surface pattern becomes the key feature, with traditional yarns and techniques combining to reinstate forgotten crafts such as embroidery and appliqué.

Crimson Flower

Size

Approximately 72cm (28⅜in) square

Materials

Rowan Felted Tweed Aran
in grey (MC),
15 x 100g (3½oz) balls

Rowan Pure Wool Aran
in light green,
1 x 100g (3½oz) ball
in sage green,
1 x 100g (3½oz) ball
in purple,
1 x 100g (3½oz) ball
in red,
1 x 100g (3½oz) ball
in pink,
1 x 100g (3½oz) ball

Square cushion pad,
76cm (30in) square

5mm (US 8) knitting needles
Knitter's sewing or tapestry needle

Tension

17 stitches and 24 rows to 10cm
(4in) square over stocking stitch when
using 5mm (US 8) knitting needles.
Adjust the needle size to achieve the
correct tension.

Everyone knows the story of Beauty and the Beast and most cultures have their own version of it. This vibrantly colourful intarsia cushion is inspired by the Russian telling of the story known as *The Enchanted Prince* or *The Crimson Flower*. Red flowers such as those featured in this design often appear in Russian folklore, where they symbolise love. Russian and Ukrainian embroideries and paintings almost always include a red flower in some form, often set against a black or dark background. A group of flowers in bright colours is a frequent motif in folk art – something to bear in mind if you would like to give your décor an authentically folkloric flavour.

Front

Using MC, cast on 125 sts.
Row 1 (RS): Knit.
Row 2: Purl.
These 2 rows set stocking stitch.
Repeat pattern as set until a total of
20 rows have been completed,
ending with a WS row.
Row 21 (RS): K15, work the first row
of chart, reading from right to left
and working the intarsia method and
changing colours as indicated, k15.
Row 22: P15, work the second row
of chart, reading from left to right
and working the intarsia method and
changing colours as indicated, p15.
Continue working as set until chart is
complete, ending with a WS row.
Starting with a knit row, and using
only MC, work in stocking stitch until
a total of 174 rows have been
completed, ending with a WS row.
Cast off.

Back

Using MC, cast on 125 sts.
Row 1 (RS): Knit.
Row 2: Purl.
These 2 rows set stocking stitch.
Repeat pattern as set until piece
measures 72cm (28⅜in) from
the cast-on edge, ending with a
WS row.
Cast off.

Finishing

Using the photograph as reference,
use light green yarn and chain stitch
to embroider the flower stems.
   Pin out the Front and Back pieces
onto a padded surface and lightly
block
   Weave in loose ends.
   Using MC and mattress stitch, sew
the Back and Front pieces together,
inserting the cushion pad into the
cover before completing the seam.

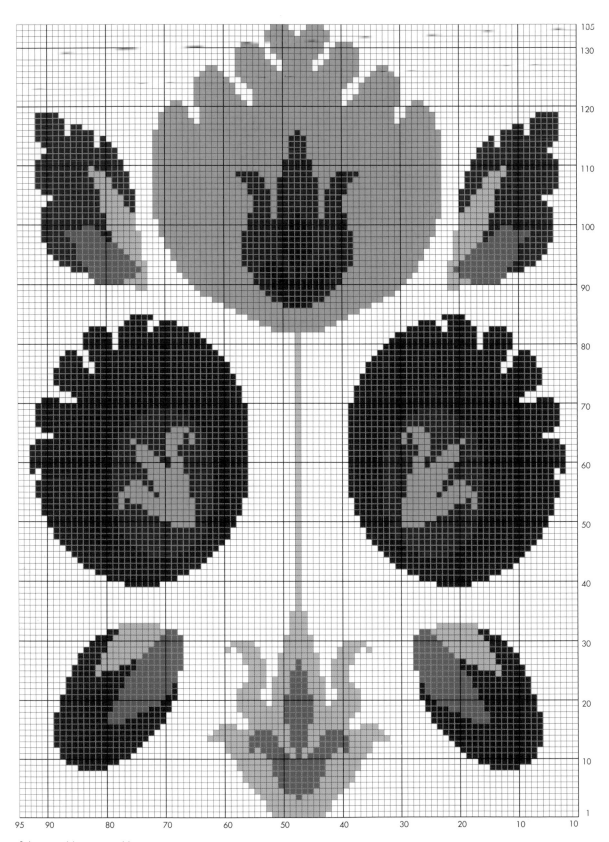

Key

☐	grey (MC), k on RS, p on WS
■	sage green, k on RS, p on WS
■	light green, k on RS, p on WS
■	purple, k on RS, p on WS
■	red, k on RS, p on WS
■	pink, k on RS, p on WS

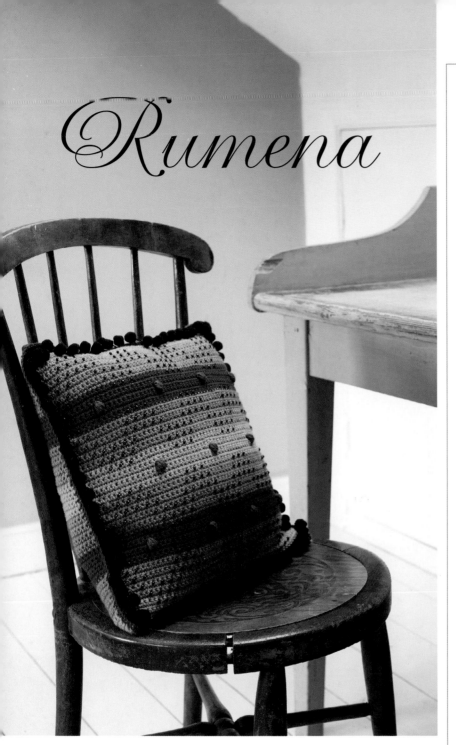

Rumena

Size
Approximately 32.5cm (13in) square

Materials
Rowan Wool Cotton
in green,
1 x 50g (1¾oz) ball
in orange,
1 x 50g (1¾oz) ball
in pink,
2 x 50g (1¾oz) balls
in red,
1 x 50g (1¾oz) ball
in grey,
1 x 50g (1¾oz) ball

Debbie Abrahams beads size 6
in black (748),
1 x 500 bead pack

Black pom pom edging,
1.5m (5ft) x 12mm (½in)
Square cushion pad,
35cm (14in) square

3.5mm (US E4) crochet hook
Knitter's sewing or tapestry needle

Tension
18 sts and 20 rows to 10cm (4in)
square over double crochet when
using a 3.5mm (US E4) crochet
hook. Adjust the hook size to achieve
the correct tension.

Special abbreviation
MB (make bobble): Work 5tr into
next st, leaving the final step of each
stitch on the hook each time (6 loops
on the hook), yrh, draw through all the
loops on the hook.

The colours and textures of this crochet cushion, which is embellished with geometric patterns of beads and bobbles and edged with a pom pom trim, are influenced by the folk traditions of Macedonia. Until the 1950s, the attire of Macedonian women was embellished with embroidery that conveyed information about a woman's social and marital status, her age, and even which village she came from. Geometric shapes and bright colours such as red (the word *rumena* means 'ripe red') and pink set alongside black are some of the key features of Macedonian folk embroidery that are reflected in this design.

Threading instructions

Thread beads onto yarn but remember that more than one ball of yarn is used and some balls will be used for the back of the cushion.

Front

FOUNDATION ROW: Using green yarn, 62ch, skip 1 ch, 1dc into each ch to end, turn. (61 sts)

Work from chart placing beads and bobbles and changing yarn colour as indicated.

Read (RS) rows from right to left and (WS) rows from left to right. Work 1tch at the beginning of each row. Start as follows:

Row 1 (RS): 1ch, 1 dc into each st, work the first row of chart, reading from right to left.

Row 2 (WS): 1ch, 1 dc into each st, work the second row of chart, reading from left to right.

Continue to work from chart until chart is complete.

Fasten off.

Back

Work in stripe pattern as for Front, omitting bobbles and beads.

Finishing

Pin out onto a padded surface and lightly block.

Weave in loose ends.

Join the Back and Front pieces together; with the wrong sides facing inwards and using red yarn, work a line of evenly spaced double crochet stitches through the edge stitches of both pieces, inserting the cushion pad into the cover before completing the round.

Pin and sew pom pom edging in place around the outer edge of the cushion.

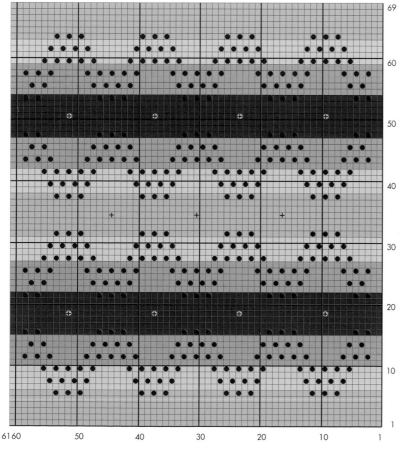

Key

- green, dc
- orange, dc
- pink, dc
- red, dc
- place bead, black
- grey, MB

Birds of Life

Size

Approximately 42cm (16½in) square

Materials

Rowan Cashsoft 4ply
in black (MC),
5 x 50g (1¾oz) balls

Small amounts of contrast colours
for embellishments,
dark pink (A)
light pink (B)
light blue (C)
dark blue (D)
green (E)

Dorset buttons or decorative buttons
for Lower Back panel,
5 x 15mm (⅝in)
Buttons,
7 x 15mm (⅝in)
Square cushion pad,
45cm (18in) square

3.25mm (US 3) knitting needles
2.5mm (US 1/0) crochet hook
Knitter's sewing or tapestry needle

Tension

25 stitches and 42 rows to 10cm
(4in) square over stocking stitch when
using 3.25mm (US 3) knitting
needles. Adjust the needle size to
achieve the correct tension.

Birds often feature in folk tales and folkloric imagery. In Middle Eastern and Asian cultures, birds are seen as symbols of immortality or as a representation of a departing or saved soul. Different birds have different connotations: the crane is a symbol of long life; the eagle typifies power; and the nightingale suggests love and longing. Traditional folk art often depicts birds and animals on either side of a central plant or tree – an idea reflected in the symmetrically arranged motifs for this cushion, in which crochet birds, flowers and leaves are set against a black moss-seed background. Such imagery can be seen to signify the tree of life, purity, and the idea of life beyond human measure.

Front

Using 3.25mm (US 3) knitting
needles and MC, cast on 107 sts.
Row 1 (RS): K1, *p1, k1; repeat
from * to end of row.
Row 2 (WS): Repeat row 1.
Repeat these two rows until piece
measures 41cm (16⅛in) from cast-on
edge ending with a RS row.
Cast off.

Lower Back panel

Using 3.25mm (US 3) knitting
needles and MC, with the RS facing,
pick up and knit 107 sts along the
cast-on edge of the Front piece.
Row 1 (WS): Purl.
Row 2 (RS): Knit.
Row 3: *P3, k5; repeat from * to
last st 3 sts, p3.
Row 4: *K3, p5; repeat from * to
last 3 sts, k3.
Row 5: Repeat row 3.
Row 6: Knit.
Row 7: P3, k1, p3, *k5, p3; repeat
from * to last 4 sts, k1, p3.
Row 8: K3, p1, *k3, p5; repeat
from * to last 7 sts, k3, p1, k3.
Row 9: Repeat row 7.
Repeat rows 2–9 until the piece
measures 30cm (12in) from cast-on

seam ending with either row 5
or row 9.
Cast off.

Upper Back panel

Using 3.25mm (US 3) knitting
needles and MC, with the RS facing,
pick up and knit 107 sts along the
cast-off edge of the Front piece.
Set moss stitch as follows:
Row 1 (WS): K1, *p1, k1; repeat
from * to end of row.
Row 2 (RS): Repeat row 1.
Repeat these two rows until piece
measures 13cm (5⅛in) from cast-on
edge, ending with a WS row.
**NEXT ROW (BUTTONHOLE CAST-OFF ROW)
(RS):** Keeping stitch pattern correct as
set work 16 sts, *cast off 3 sts,
keeping stitch pattern correct as set
and counting the st on the right-hand
needle after the last buttonhole, work
15 sts; repeat from * to last st, k1.
(5 buttonholes)
NEXT ROW (BUTTONHOLE CAST-ON ROW):
Keeping stitch pattern correct as set
work 16 sts, *turn, using the cable
method and wrapping the final stitch,
cast on 3 sts, turn, keeping stitch
pattern correct as set work 15 sts;
repeat from * to last st, k1. (107 sts)

Continue in stitch pattern as set until piece measures 17cm (6¾in) from cast-on seam ending with a RS row. Cast off.

Large crochet flower (make 1)

FOUNDATION RING: Using 2.5mm (US 1-0) crochet hook and A, 6ch, join with a ss to form a ring.

ROUND 1: 1ch, 16dc into centre of ring, ss to join to first dc.

ROUND 2: 6ch (counts as 1tr, 3ch), skip st at base of beg-6ch and 1 dc, *1tr into next st, 3ch, skip 1 st; repeat from * 7 times more, ss to join to third ch of beg-6ch.

ROUND 3: 1ch, *[1dc, 1htr, 5tr, 1htr, 1dc] into next 1ch-sp; repeat from * 7 times more, ss to join to first dc. (8 petals)

Fasten off A, Join in B in st-sp between 2dc.

ROUND 4: Working behind existing petals, *6ch, 1dc in st-sp between next 2dc at beginning/end of petal made on previous round; repeat from * 7 times more, ss to join to first dc.

ROUND 5: 1ch, [1dc, 1htr, 7tr, 1htr, 1dc] into next 6ch-sp; repeat from * 7 times more, ss to join to beg-1ch. (8 petals)

Fasten off.

Small crochet flower (make 3)

FOUNDATION RING: Using 2.5mm (US 1-0) crochet hook and A, 6ch, join with a ss to form a ring.

ROUND 1: 1ch, 12dc into centre of ring, ss to join to first dc.

ROUND 2: 3ch, skip st at base of beg-3ch and 1 dc, 1dc into next st, 3ch, *skip 1 dc, 1dc into next st, 3ch; repeat from * 4 times more, ss to join to beg-1ch.

Fasten off A. Join in B to 3ch-sp.

ROUND 3: 1ch, [1dc, 1htr, 3tr, 1htr,

1dc] into same 3ch-sp, [1dc, 1htr, 3tr, 1htr, 1dc] into each of remaining spaces to end of round, ss to join to beg-1ch. (6 petals)
Fasten off.

Five-leaf crochet piece (make 1)

Using 2.5mm (US 1-0) hook throughout and E.

LEAF 1: 20ch, skip 2 ch, 1dc into each next 2 ch, 1htr into next ch, 1tr into each next 2 ch, 1dtr into each next 2 ch, dtr2tog, 1tr into each next 3 ch, 1htr into next ch, ss into each next 5 ch, do not turn.

LEAF 2: Work as leaf 1.

LEAF 3: 20ch, skip 2 ch, 1dc into each next 2 ch, 1htr into next ch, 1tr into each next 2 ch, 1dtr into each next 4 ch, 1tr into each next 3 ch, 1htr into next ch, ss into each next 5 ch, do not turn.

LEAF 4: 19ch, skip 2 ch, 1dc into each next 2 ch, 1htr into next ch, 1tr into each next 2 ch, 2dtr into each next 2 ch, 2dtr into next ch, 1tr into each next 3 ch, 1htr into next ch, ss into each next 5 ch, do not turn.

LEAF 5: Work as leaf 4, do not fasten off.

BASE: 1ch, 1dc into st at base of each 5 leaves, 5ch, turn, 1dtr into each st, holding back the last step of each st to leave 6 loops on the hook, yrh, draw through all loops, 1ch.
Fasten off.

Small leaf (make 2)

FOUNDATION CHAIN: Using 2.5mm (US 1-0) crochet hook and E, 11ch.
ROUND 1: Skip 1 ch, 1dc into next ch, 1htr into next ch, 1tr into each next 2 ch, 1dtr into next ch, 2dtr into next ch, 1dtr into next ch, 1tr into next ch, 1htr into next ch, 1dc into next ch, 1ch, working along base of foundation chain, 1dc into next ch, 1htr into next ch, 1tr into next ch, 1dtr into next ch, 2dtr into next ch, 1dtr into next ch, 1tr into each next 2 ch, 1htr into next ch, 1dc into final ch, ss into side of tch, 1ch.
Fasten off.

Bird one (make 1)

FOUNDATION CHAIN: Using 2.5mm (US 1-0) crochet hook and C, 35ch.
ROW 1: Skip 1 ch, 1dc into each next 3 ch, 1htr into each next 2 ch, *2tr into next ch, 1tr into next ch; repeat from * 4 times more, 1 tr into each next 7 ch, [tr2tog over next 2 ch] 3 times, 1htr into each next 2 ch, 1dc into each next 3 ch, ss into last ch, turn.
ROW 2: 1ch, skip 1 ch, ss into each next 2 sts, 1dc into each next 2 sts, 1htr into each next 2 sts, tr3tog, 1tr into each next 4 sts, *2tr into next st, 1tr into next st; repeat from * 5 times more, 1tr into each next 4 sts, 1htr into each next 2 sts, 1dc into each next 3 sts, ss into next st, skip last st, turn.
ROW 3: 1ch, skip 1 ch and 1 ss, ss into next st, 1dc into each next 2 sts, 1htr into each next 2 sts, * 1tr into next st, 2tr into next st; repeat from * 8 times more, 1tr into next st, 1htr into each next 2 sts, 1dc into each next 2 sts, ss into next st.
Fasten off. Do not turn. Join in D into 1ch at beg of last row.
ROW 4: 1ch, 1dc into 1dc of row 1, 1dc into st at end of row 2, 1dc into ss at beg of last row, 1dc into each next 3 sts, 1htr into each next 2 sts, 1tr into next st, 2tr into next st, *1tr into each next 2 sts, 2tr into next st; repeat from * 6 times more, 1tr into each next 9 sts, 1tr into dc on row 2, tr3tog, 1htr into each next 2 sts, 1dc into each next 2 sts, ss into each next 2 sts.
Fasten off.

Wing for Bird one (make 1)

FOUNDATION CHAIN: Using 2.5mm (US 1-0) crochet hook and D, 11ch.
ROUND 1: Skip 1 ch, 1dc into next ch, 1htr into next ch, 1tr into each next 2 ch, 1dtr into next ch, 2dtr into next ch, 1dtr into next ch, 1tr into next ch, 1htr into next ch, 1dc into next ch, 1ch, working along base of foundation chain, 1dc into next ch, 1htr into next ch, 1tr into next ch, 1dtr into each next 2 ch, 1tr into each next ch, 1htr into next ch, 1dc into next ch, ss into each next 2 ch, ss into tip of wing.
Fasten off.

Experiment with decorative trimmings as an alternative means of adornment.

Bird two (make 1)

FOUNDATION CHAIN: Using 2.5mm (US 1-0) crochet hook and C, 35ch.

ROW 1: Skip 1 ch, ss into next st, 1dc into each next 3 ch, 1htr into each next 2 ch, [tr2tog over next 2 ch] 3 times, 1tr into each next 7 ch, *1tr into next ch, 2tr into next ch; repeat from * 4 times more, 1htr into each next 2 ch, 1dc into each next 3 ch, turn.

ROW 2: 1ch, skip 1 dc, ss into next st, 1dc into each next 3 sts, 1htr into each next 2 sts, 1tr into each next 4 sts, *1tr into next st, 2tr into next st; repeat from * 5 times more, 1tr into each next 4 sts, tr3tog, 1htr into each next 2 sts, 1dc into each next 2 sts, ss into each next 2 sts, turn.

ROW 3: 1ch, skip 1 ch and 1 ss, ss into each next 8 sts, 1dc into each next 2 sts, 1htr into each next 2 sts, 1tr into next st, *2tr into next st, 1tr into next st; repeat from * 8 times more, 1htr into each next 2 sts, 1dc into each next 2 sts, ss into each next 2 sts. Fasten off. Do not turn. Join in D into 1ch at beg of last row.

ROW 4: Ss into each next 2 sts, 1dc into each next 2 sts, 1htr into each next 2 sts, tr3tog, 1tr into each next 10 sts, *2tr into next st, 1tr into each next 2 sts; repeat from * 6 times more, 2tr into next st, 1tr into next st, 1htr into each next 2 sts, 1dc into each next 3 sts, 1dc into ss at beg of last row, 1dc into st at end of row 2, 1dc into 1st dc of row 1. Fasten off.

Wing for Bird two (make 1)

FOUNDATION CHAIN: Using 2.5mm (US 1-0) crochet hook and D, 11ch.

ROUND 1: Skip 1 ch, ss into each next 2 ch, 1dc into next ch, 1htr into next ch, 1tr into each next ch, 1dtr into each next 2 ch, 1tr into next ch, 1htr into next ch, 1dc into next ch, 1ch, working along base of foundation chain, 1dc into next ch, 1htr into next ch, 1tr into next ch, 1dtr into next ch, 2dtr into next ch, 1dtr into next ch, 1tr into each next 2 ch, 1htr into next ch, 1dc into next ch, ss into tip of wing.
Fasten off.

Finishing

Pin out the Front and Back pieces onto a padded surface and lightly block.

Using the photograph as reference, sew crochet pieces in place on front cushion piece.

Using D and C, embroider chain stitch to represent the birds' tails.

Attach buttons into the centre of Large flower and in two groups of three near Five-leaf crochet piece.

Using MC, work a French knot to represent birds' eyes.

Using E, work satin stitch across the Bird shapes to represent a beak.

Sew wings into place, leaving the tip of the wing unattached.

Using MC and mattress stitch, sew the side seams. Weave loose ends into the seam stitches.

Attach Dorset buttons (see Techniques Guide, p93) or decorative buttons to Lower Back panel and secure in line with buttonholes.

Little
Red Cap

Jacob and Wilhelm Grimm collected and published folklore in the form of *Grimms' Fairy Tales*, the first of which were published in 1812. The Brothers Grimm, as they are better known, are among the most renowned storytellers of European folk tales; many of the original stories were dark, violent and frightening, with a strong moral theme. The Grimms' work popularised stories such as *Cinderella*, *Rapunzel* and *Little Red Riding Hood* – or *Little Red Cap*, as the heroine was originally known, and after whom this cushion design is named. Featuring a grey and red abstract geometrical motif created using the Fair Isle technique, this cushion combines knitted pieces with a central crochet medallion.

Size
Approximately 50cm (20in) diameter

Materials
Rowan Wool Cotton
in red (MC),
5 x 50g (1¾oz) balls
in grey (CC),
2 x 50g (1¾oz) balls

Small amount of waste DK-weight yarn

Round cushion pad
56cm (22in) diameter

4mm (US 6) knitting needles
3.5mm (US E4) crochet hook
Knitter's sewing or tapestry needle

Tension
22 stitches and 30 rows to 10cm (4in) square over stocking stitch when using 4mm (US 6) knitting needles. Adjust the needle size to achieve the correct tension.

Special abbreviations
MB (make bobble): Work 5tr into next st, leaving the final step of each stitch on the hook each time (6 loops on the hook), yrh, draw through all loops.

Back
Using 4mm (US 6) knitting needles and waste yarn, cast on 47 sts.
Knit one row.
Purl one row.
Fasten off waste yarn. Join in MC.
Row 1 (RS): Knit.
Row 2: Purl.
Row 3: Knit 42 sts, wrap the next stitch, turn.
Rows 4, 6, 8, 10, 12, 14 AND 16: Purl.
Row 5: Knit 37 sts, wrap the next stitch, turn.

Row 7: Knit 32 sts, wrap the next stitch, turn.

Row 9: Knit 27 sts, wrap the next stitch, turn.

Row 11: Knit 22 sts, wrap the next stitch, turn.

Row 13: Knit 17 sts, wrap the next stitch, turn.

Row 15: Knit 12 sts, wrap the next stitch, turn.

Row 17 (RS): Knit across the row, moving wrapping strands to the WS by inserting the right-hand needle under the wrap, then into the wrapped stitch and knitting the two together.

Row 18: Purl.

Repeat rows 1–18, 22 times more. (23 pattern repeats)

Repeat rows 1–17, once more.

Fasten off MC. Join in waste yarn.

Next row (WS): Purl.

Cast off.

Front

Using 4mm (US 6) knitting needles and waste yarn, cast on 47 sts.

Knit one row.

Purl one row.

Fasten off waste yarn. Join in MC and CC.

Starting from row 3, work from chart using the Fair Isle technique, changing colours and wrapping stitches as indicated until the chart is complete.

**Repeat the chart starting with row 1, knit across the row, moving wrapping strands to the WS and changing colours as indicated.

Repeat from ** 22 times more. (24 pattern repeats)

Repeat row 1 of chart, knit across the row, moving wrapping strands to the WS and changing colours as indicated.

Fasten off MC. Join in waste yarn.

Next row (WS): Purl.

Cast off.

Back crochet medallion

Foundation ring: Using 3.5mm (US E4) crochet hook and MC, 6ch, join with a ss to form a ring.

Round 1: 3ch (counts as 1tr), work 13tr into centre of ring, ss to join to top of beg-3ch. (14 sts)

Round 2: 3ch (counts as 1tr), 1tr into st at base of beg-3ch, 2tr into each st to end of round, ss to join to top of beg-3ch. (28 sts)

Round 3: 3ch (counts as 1tr), skip st at base of beg-3ch, *2tr into next st, 1tr into next st; repeat from * until 1 st rem, 2tr into next st, ss to join to top of beg-3ch. (42 sts)

Round 4: 3ch (counts as 1tr), skip st at base of beg-3ch, 1tr into next st, *2tr into next st, 1tr into next 2 sts; repeat from * until 1 st rem, 2tr into next st, ss to join to top of beg-3ch. (56 sts)

Round 5: 3ch (counts as 1tr), skip st at base of beg-3ch, 1tr into each next 2 sts, *2tr into next st, 1tr into each next 3 sts; repeat from * until 1 st rem, 2tr into next st, ss to join to top of beg-3ch. (70 sts)

Fasten off.

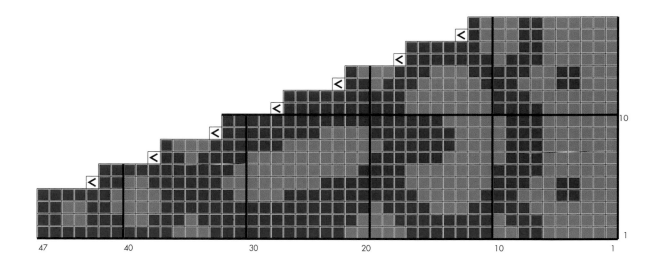

47   40   30   20   10   1

10

1

Front crochet medallion

FOUNDATION RING: Using 3.5mm (US E4) crochet hook and MC, 6ch, join with a ss to form a ring.

ROUND 1: 3ch (counts as 1tr), work 13tr into centre of ring, ss to join to top of beg-3ch. (14 sts)

ROUND 2: 3ch (counts as 1tr), 1tr into st at base of beg-3ch, 2tr into each st to end of round, ss to join to top of beg-3ch. (28 sts)

ROUND 3: Using MC, 1ch, *1dc into next st, 2dc into next st, 1dc into next st, using CC work bobble into next st, using MC repeat from * to end of round, ss to join to top of beg-1ch. (35 sts)

ROUND 4: 3ch (counts as 1tr), skip st at base of beg-3ch, *1tr into next st, 2tr into next st; repeat from * to end of round, ss to join to top of beg-3ch. (52 sts)

ROUND 5: 3ch (counts as 1tr), skip st at base of beg-3ch, 1tr into each next 2 sts, *using CC work 2tr into next st, using MC 1tr into each of next 3 sts; repeat from * until 1 st rem, using CC work 2tr into next st, ss to join to top of beg-3ch. (65 sts)

ROUND 6: 1ch, 1dc into each next 4 sts, *2dc into next st, 1dc into each next 4 sts; repeat from * until 1 st rem, 2dc into next st, ss to join. (78 sts)

Finishing

Complete the Back piece by threading MC into a knitter's needle or tapestry needle and grafting the first row of MC knitting to the last row of MC knitting to create an invisible seam. Unravel the waste yarn. Repeat for the Front piece but sew in the row according to the chart row 2.

Pin out the Back and Front pieces onto a padded surface and lightly block.

Attach Back crochet medallion to centre of the Back piece.

Attach Front crochet medallion to centre of Front piece.

Weave in loose ends.

Using MC and mattress stitch, sew the Back and Front pieces together, inserting the cushion pad into the cover before completing the seam.

Key

■ red (MC), k on RS, p on WS
▨ grey (CC), k on RS, p on WS
< wrap stitch

Troika

The Russian and Bulgarian word *troika* has several meanings, one of which refers to a lavishly embellished sled or carriage drawn by three horses harnessed side by side. Horses often feature in folklore, with richly decorated saddles and plaited manes. Pom poms are frequently used in the traditional decoration of bridles and tack, and on a smaller scale to adorn traditional folk costume and home interiors.

Pom poms make a joyful addition to many soft furnishings; here they are used to edge a textured crochet cushion.

Size
Approximately 42cm (16½in) square

Materials
Rowan Felted Tweed Aran
in grey (MC),
5 x 100g (3½oz) balls

For pom poms:
Rowan Pure Wool Aran
in purple,
1 x 100g (3½oz) ball
in pink,
1 x 100g (3½oz) ball
in red,
1 x 100g (3½oz) ball
in sage green,
1 x 100g (3½oz) ball
in light green,
1 x 100g (3½oz) ball

Square cushion pad,
45cm (18in) square

5.5mm (US 19) crochet hook
Knitter's sewing or tapestry needle

Tension
14 sts and 11 rows to 10cm (4in) square over pattern repeat when using a 5.5mm (US 19) crochet hook. Adjust the hook size to achieve the correct tension.

Note
The left-over yarn from the Crimson Flower floor cushion cover (page 14) will be enough to make the 5cm (2in) pom poms used for this project.

Back and Front (both alike)
FOUNDATION ROW: Using MC, 61ch, skip 1 ch, 1dc into each ch to end, turn. (60 sts)
Row 1 (RS): 1ch, *1dc into back loop of next st, 1dc into front loop of next st; repeat from * to end of row, turn.
Repeat row 1 until piece measures 42cm (16½in) from foundation-chain edge, ending with a RS row.
Fasten off.

Finishing
Pin out onto a padded surface and lightly block.

Weave in loose ends.

Join the Back and Front pieces together; with the wrong sides facing inwards, work double crochet stitches evenly spaced through both edges, inserting the cushion pad into the cover before completing the round.

Make four, 5cm (2in), pom poms in each of the contrast colours. (20 pom poms in total.)

Using the photograph as reference, sew the pom poms to the cushion seams, ensuring that they are evenly spaced and well secured.

Gretel

Hansel and Gretel tells the story of siblings who are forced into the forest by their cruel stepmother in the hope that they will get lost, giving her two fewer mouths to feed. A witch in the forest lures the children to her cottage, which is made of brightly coloured sweets and biscuits. She enslaves Gretel and fattens up Hansel with the plan of eventually eating him. The children use their wiles to trick the witch and return home, after which, of course, they live happily ever after.

This rug takes inspiration from the vivid candy colours of the witch's house; it is made up of crochet motifs that are felted to form a hardwearing fabric.

Size

Approximately 110 x 85cm (43⅜ x 33½in)

Materials

Rowan Big Wool
in pink (A),
2 x 100g (3½oz) balls
in red (B),
2 x 100g (3½oz) balls
in orange (C),
3 x 100g (3½oz) balls
in light green (D),
2 x 100g (3½oz) balls
in dark green (E),
1 x 100g (3½oz) ball

Small amount of matching lighter-weight yarn for stitching the motifs together.

10mm (US N/P15) crochet hook
Knitter's sewing or tapestry needle

Tension

Before washing

One seven-petal flower measures approximately 22.5cm (11in) across the diameter when using a 10mm (US N/P15) crochet hook. Adjust the crochet hook size to achieve the correct tension.

After washing

One seven-petal flower measures approximately 19cm (7½in) across the diameter when using a 10mm (US N/P15) crochet hook. Adjust the crochet hook size to achieve the correct tension.

Note

Join in a new yarn into a stitch a short distance from where the last yarn was fastened off.

Seven-petal flower (make 8)

FOUNDATION RING: Using A, 6ch, join with a ss to form a ring.

ROUND 1: 3ch, (counts as 1tr) work 13tr into centre of ring, ss to join to top of beg-3ch. (14 sts)
Fasten off A. Join in B.

ROUND 2: 1ch (counts as 1dc), 1dc into the tr at base of beg-3ch, work 2dc into each tr to end of round, ss to join to top of beg-3ch. (28 sts)
Fasten off B. Join in C.

ROUND 3: 7ch (counts as 1tr, 4ch), *skip 3 ch, 1dc into next ch, 1tr into each of next 3 ch, skip 3 dc, 1dc into next dc, 7ch; repeat from * 6 times more, ss to join to first ch of beg-7ch.

ROUND 4: 1ch, 1dc at base of beg-1ch, 1dc into base of each next 3 ch, *3dc into sp created between tch and first dc, 1dc into next dc, 1dc into each next 3 tr, 1dc into next dc, 1dc into base of each next 4 ch; repeat from * 5 times more, work 3dc into sp created between tch and first dc, 1dc into next dc, 1dc into each next 3 tr, ss to join to beg-1ch.
Fasten off.

Six-petal flower (make 11)

FOUNDATION RING: Using D, 2ch, work 6dc into first ch, join with a ss to first dc to form a ring.

ROUND 1: 1ch, 2dc into each st to end of round. (12 sts)

ROUND 2: 4ch (counts as 1tr, 1ch), *1tr into next dc, 1ch; rep from * to end of round, ss to join to third ch of beg-4ch.

Fasten off A. Join in C into 1ch-sp.

ROUND 3: 2dc into sp at base of join, 3dc each 1ch-sp to end of round, ss to join to first dc. (36 sts)

Fasten off C. Join in A into top of dc.

ROUND 4: 1ch (counts as 1dc), *1htr into next dc, 2tr into next dc, 1dtr into next dc, 2tr into next dc, 1htr into next dc, 1dc into next dc, rep from * 5 times more, ss to join to first ch of beg-1ch.

Fasten off A. Join in B into a dc of Round 3 below a dc on Round 4. Working into rounds 3 and 4 as required.

ROUND 5: *[1dc into next st on round 4, 1ch] 6 times, 1dc into next st on round 5, 1dc into next dc on round 3; rep from * 4 times more, [1dc into next st on round 4, 1ch] 6 times, 1dc into next st on round 4, ss to join to first dc.

Fasten off.

Leaves (make 6)

FOUNDATION CHAIN: Using E, 11ch.

ROUND 1: Skip 3 ch, *[1tr into next ch, 1ch] twice, [1dtr into next ch, 1ch] twice, [1tr into next ch, 1ch] twice, ** work 2dc into first ch, 1ch, working along base of foundation ch, skip 1 ch; rep from * to **, 1ch, skip 1 ch, ss into next ch, 1ch.

Fasten off E. Join in D into first 1ch-sp created by the previous round, to the left side of the 2dc at tip.

ROUND 2: 3ch (counts as 1tr), 1tr into 1ch-sp at base of beg-3ch, [2tr into next 1ch-sp] 6 times, 3ch, skip 2 ch, ss into next ch, [2tr into next 1ch-sp] 7 times, ss to join to top of beg-3ch.

Fasten off.

Finishing

Weave in loose ends.

Using the position guide below as reference, join pieces together using small stitches in matching yarn.

Machine felting is not an exact science. Wash on a short 30-degree machine cycle without any detergent.

Gently pull and ease the motifs into shape and dry flat.

If the felting process has not been as successful as hoped for, repeat the same machine cycle or put it in on a hotter cycle that involves more turbulence and add a little detergent. Placing your crochet pieces in the machine with other items such as towels or jeans will add agitation and aid the felting process.

Be bold with your choice of colours to create a lively interior.

Use this illustration for reference when joining the crochet pieces.

Babouchka

The matryoshka doll is a popular Russian folkloric item, first made in 1890. The colourful wooden dolls decrease in size, each layer hiding away a smaller doll. The largest and outermost doll is usually depicted as a woman; the dolls inside can be of either gender, and the smallest and final doll is usually a baby. These are also known as babouchka dolls – *babouchka* being the Russian for 'grandmother' or 'old lady'; they are often painted wearing folk costumes and have a rather maternal look about them.

This crochet bedspread celebrates the babouchka, with its interlocking, interconnecting crochet motifs and characteristic folkloric colours of red, white and pink.

Size
Approximately 130 x 185cm (51 x 73in)

Materials
Rowan Wool Cotton
in cream (A),
8 x 50g (1¾oz) balls
in bright pink (B),
5 x 50g (1¾oz) balls
in red (C),
8 x 50g (1¾oz) balls
in light pink (D),
10 x 50g (1¾oz) balls
in brown (E),
3 x 50g (1¾oz) balls

in grey (F),
3 x 50g (1¾oz) balls

Amy Butler Belle Organic DK
in green (G),
2 x 50g (1¾oz) balls
in yellow (H),
2 x 50g (1¾oz) balls
in purple (I),
3 x 50g (1¾oz) balls

3.5mm (US E4) crochet hook
Knitter's sewing or tapestry needle

Tension
One hexagon measures approximately 13.75cm (5⅜in) from tip to tip when using a 3.5mm (US E4) crochet hook. Adjust the crochet hook size to achieve the correct tension.

Colourway one (make 82)
FOUNDATION RING: Using A, 6ch, join with a ss to form a ring.
ROUND 1: 3ch, tr2tog into ring (counts as tr3tog), 3ch, [tr3tog, 3ch] 5 times, ss to join to top of beg-3ch. Fasten off A. Join in B into sp created by last 3ch.
ROUND 2: 3ch, tr2tog into same 3ch-sp, (counts as tr3tog), 3ch *[tr3tog, 3ch, tr3tog] into next 3ch-sp, 3ch; repeat from * 4 times

more, tr3tog, 3ch, into next 3ch-sp, 3ch, ss to join to top of beg-3ch. Fasten off B. Join in C into sp created by last 3ch.
ROUND 3: 3ch, tr2tog into same 3ch-sp, (counts as tr3tog), 3ch, *[tr3tog, 3ch, tr3tog] into next 3ch-sp, 3ch, tr3tog into next 3ch-sp, 3ch; repeat from * 4 times more, [tr3tog, 3ch, tr3tog] into next 3ch-sp, 3ch, ss to join to top of beg-3ch.
Fasten off C. Join in D into sp created

by last 3ch.
ROUND 4: 3ch (counts as 1tr), 1tr into same 3ch-sp, *3tr into next 3ch-sp, [3tr, 2ch, 3tr] into next 3ch-sp, 3tr into next 3ch-sp; repeat from * 4 times more, 3tr into next 3ch-sp, [3tr, 2ch, 3tr] into next 3ch-sp, 1tr into same sp as 3ch at beg of round, ss to join to top of beg-3ch.
Fasten off D. Join in A.
ROUND 5: 1ch, 1dc into each next 8 sts, *work 2dc into 2ch-sp, 1dc

Colourway four (make 8)

Work as for colourway one but in the following yarns.

FOUNDATION CHAIN AND ROUND 1: H.
ROUND 2: B.
ROUND 3: I.
ROUND 4: E.
ROUND 5: F.

Colourway five (make 48)

Work as for colourway one but in the following yarns.

FOUNDATION CHAIN AND ROUND 1: B.
ROUND 2: C.
ROUND 3: I.
ROUND 4: E.
ROUND 5: F.

Finishing

Pin out onto a padded surface and lightly block.

Join the hexagons, using the position guide as reference. Position neighbouring hexagons with wrong sides facing. Then, using yarn A to join all the light-coloured hexagons and yarn H to join the darker-coloured hexagons, work a line of evenly spaced double crochet stitches through the edge stitches of both hexagons.

Weave loose ends into the seam stitches.

into each next 12 sts; repeat from * 4 times more, 1dc into each next 4 sts, ss to join to top of beg-1ch. Fasten off.

Colourway two (make 15)

Work as for colourway one but in the following yarns.

FOUNDATION CHAIN AND ROUND 1: G.
ROUND 2: B.
ROUND 3: C.
ROUND 4: D.
ROUND 5: A.

Colourway three (make 15)

Work as for colourway one but in the following yarns.

FOUNDATION CHAIN AND ROUND 1: G.
ROUND 2: H.
ROUND 3: A.
ROUND 4: D.
ROUND 5: A.

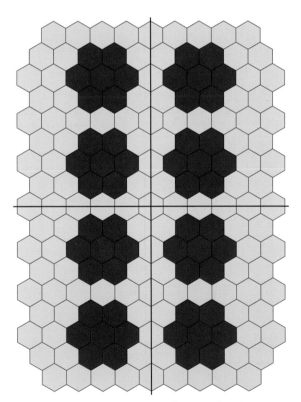

Use this illustration for reference when joining the crochet motifs together.

Paprika

Travel for trade and commerce from around the 16th century took explorers to remote lands to experience new cultures. As well as tales of foreign people and customs, they often returned home with riches unknown in their own lands, including spices, which were a rare and therefore very expensive luxury commodity. These herbs and spices brought unfamiliar heat and vibrant colours into cooking, and they retain their prized place in the spice racks of today's kitchens. Some of the first spices to prove their popularity were paprika and chilli powder.

This vivid crochet cushion is inspired by the hot colours of spices such as paprika, featuring clashing bands of orange, red and bright green. The front and back panels are made in different colourways.

Size
Approximately 72cm (28in) square

Materials
Rowan Handknit Cotton
in navy (A),
4 x 50g (1¾oz) balls
in burgandy (B),
4 x 50g (1¾oz) balls
in bright green (C),
3 x 50g (1¾oz) balls
in yellow (D),
3 x 50g (1¾oz) balls
in red (E),
4 x 50g (1¾oz) balls
in orange (F),
4 x 50g (1¾oz) balls

Square cushion pad,
76cm (30in) square

4mm (US H-8) crochet hook
Knitter's sewing or tapestry needle

Tension
15 sts and 17 rows to 10cm (4in) square over double crochet when using a 4mm (US H-8) crochet hook. Adjust the needle size to achieve the correct tension.

Front (make 6 strips)
FOUNDATION ROW: Using A, 110ch, skip 1 ch, 1dc into each ch to end, turn. (109 sts)
ROW 1 (WS): 1ch, 1dc into next st, *1htr into next st, 1tr into next st, 3dtr into next st, 1tr into next st, 1htr into next st, 1dc into next st; rep from * 18 times, join in C on the final

step of the last stitch, turn. (131 sts)
ROW 2 (RS): 1ch, dc2tog over first 2 sts, 1dc into each of next 2 sts, *3dc into next st, 1dc into each of next 2 sts, dc3tog over next 3 sts, 1dc into each of next 2 sts; rep from * 9 times, 3dc into next st, 1dc into each of next 2 sts, dc2tog over last 2 sts, join in D on the final step of the

last stitch, turn. (131sts)

Row 3: Repeat row 2, join in B on the final step of the last stitch, turn.

Row 4: 4ch (counts as 1dtr), skip st at base of beg-4ch, 1dtr into next st, *1tr into next st, 1htr into next st, 1dc into next st, 1htr into next st, 1tr into next st, dtr3tog over next 3 sts; rep from * 16 times, 1tr into next st, 1htr into next st, 1dc into next st, 1htr into next st, 1tr into next st, dtr2tog over last 2 sts, turn.

Row 5: 1ch, 1dc into each st to end, miss tch, join in F on the final step of the last stitch, turn. (109 sts)

Row 6: 1ch, 1dc into each st to end, join in E on the final step of the last stitch, turn.

Row 7: Repeat row 6, join in A on the final step of the last stitch, turn.

Row 8: Repeat row 6.

Row 9: Repeat row 1, join in C on the final step of the last stitch, turn.

Row 10: Repeat row 2, join in D on the final step of the last stitch, turn.

Row 11: Repeat row 2, join in B on the final step of the last stitch, turn.

Row 12: Repeat row 4.

Row 13: Repeat row 5.

Fasten off.

Join with dc on reverse side using alternate colours; orange to join strip 1 to strip 2, then red to join strip 2 to 3, orange 3 to 4, red 4 to 5 and orange 5 to 6.

Back (make 6 strips)

FOUNDATION ROW: Using E, 110ch, skip 1 ch, 1dc into each ch to end, turn. (109 sts)

Row 1 (WS): 1ch, 1dc into next st, *1htr into next st, 1tr into next st, 3dtr into next st, 1tr into next st, 1htr into next st, 1dc into next st; rep from * 18 times, join in C on the final step of the last stitch, turn. (131 sts)

Row 2 (RS): 1ch, dc2tog over first 2 sts, 1dc into each of next 2 sts, *3dc into next st, 1dc into each of next 2 sts, dc3tog over next 3 sts, 1dc into each of next 2 sts; rep from * 9 times, 3dc into next st, 1dc into each of next 2 sts, dc2tog over last 2 sts, join in D on the final step of the last stitch, turn. (131sts)

Row 3: Repeat row 2, join in F on the final step of the last stitch, turn.

Row 4: 4ch (counts as 1dtr), skip st at base of beg-4ch, 1dtr into next st, *1tr into next st, 1htr into next st, 1dc into next st, 1htr into next st, 1tr into next st, dtr3tog over next 3 sts; rep from * 16 times, 1tr into next st, 1htr into next st, 1dc into next st, 1htr into next st, 1tr into next st, dtr2tog over last 2 sts, turn.

Row 5: 1ch, 1dc into each st to end, miss tch, join in B on the final step of the last stitch, turn. (109 sts)

Row 6: 1ch, 1dc into each st to end, join in A on the final step of the last stitch, turn.

Row 7: Repeat row 6, join in E on the final step of the last stitch, turn.

Row 8: Repeat row 6.

Row 9: Repeat row 1, join in C on the final step of the last stitch, turn.

Row 10: Repeat row 2, join in D on the final step of the last stitch, turn.

Row 11: Repeat row 2, join in F on the final step of the last stitch, turn.

Row 12: Repeat row 4.

Row 13: Repeat row 5.

Fasten off.

Join with dc on reverse side using alternate colours; burgundy to join strip 1 to strip 2, then navy to join strip 2 to 3, burgundy 3 to 4, navy 4 to 5 and burgundy 5 to 6.

Finishing

Pin out onto a padded surface and lightly block.

Weave in loose ends.

Join the Back and Front pieces together; with the wrong sides facing inwards, using B, work a line of evenly spaced double crochet stitches through the edge stitches of both pieces, inserting the cushion pad into the cover before completing the round.

Intricate details and abundant surface pattern are key to the folk aesthetic.

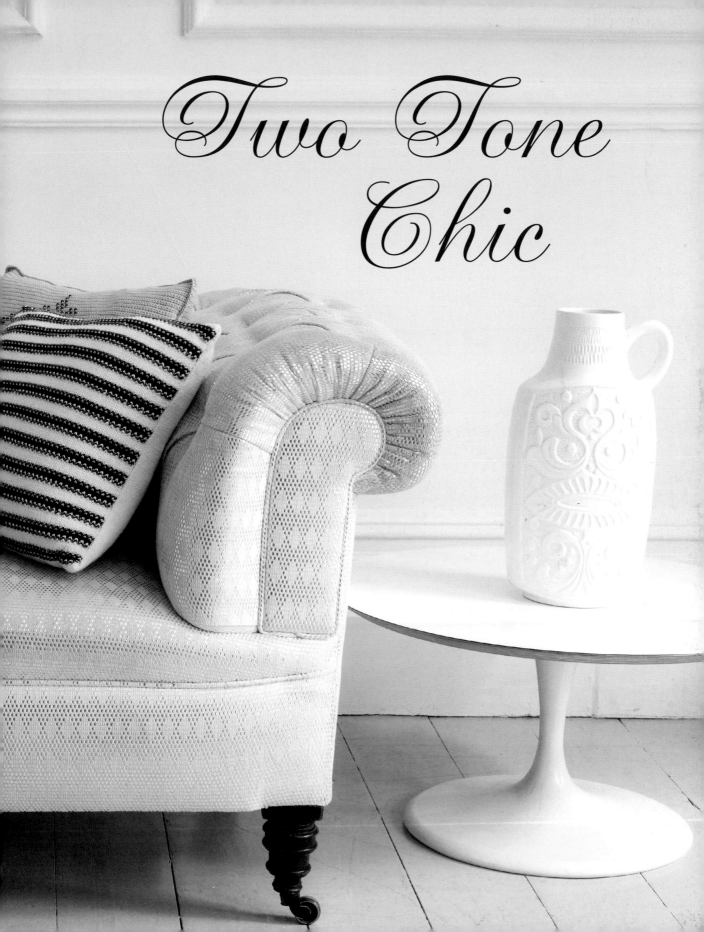

Two Tone Chic

This story is sophisticated and timeless, with a hint of femininity. It pays homage to the designs of Coco Chanel and Paul Poiret, who triumphed with the simplified fashion and interior design trends of the early part of the twentieth century. Monochrome tones of black, grey, taupe, cream and white are the inspiration for this design story, which has been based on geometric patterns and art deco interiors. Pieces are timeless, with the seemingly simple designs emphasising stitch detail and added decoration in the shape of buttons, beads and ribbons. All of these designs would work well in any interior setting and could be reworked in alternative colour combinations to create a different mood.

Gabrielle

Size

Approximately 43 x 55cm
(17 x 21⅞in)
Will stretch to fit pillow
50 x 75cm (20 x 29½in)

Materials

Rowan Siena Cotton 4ply
in cream,
6 x 50g (1¾oz) balls

Vintage shirt buttons,
14 x 12mm (½in)
Vintage shirt buttons,
16 x 10mm (⅜in)
Black ribbon,
3m (10ft) x 7mm (¼in)

2.5mm (US B1/C2) crochet hook
Knitter's sewing or tapestry needle

Tension

14 pattern repeats [1tr, 1ch] and
11 rows to 10cm (4in) square when
using a 2.5mm (US B1/C2) crochet
hook. Adjust the hook size to achieve
the correct tension.

The celebrated fashion designer Gabrielle 'Coco' Chanel had a tough childhood: her mother died when she was 12 and her father abandoned the family. She spent more than five years at the monastery of Aubazine, where she trained to become a seamstress and was recognised for her excellent sewing skills. Gabrielle loved to sew and from a very early age showed a natural ability to turn fabrics into finely crafted pieces.

This beautiful crochet pillowcase slip pays homage to Gabrielle's fine sewing skills. A simple mesh-stitch pattern forms the main section, which is subtly embellished with a lacy edging, a contrasting narrow ribbon and vintage buttons.

Back and Front (both alike)

FOUNDATION ROW: 94ch, skip 3 ch (counts as 1tr), work 1tr into fourth ch from hook, *1ch, skip 1 ch, 1tr into next ch; rep from * to last ch, 1tr into the same ch as the last tr, turn.
Row 1 (WS): 4ch (counts as 1tr, 1ch), skip 2 tr of previous row, 1tr into 1ch-sp, *1ch, 1tr into next 1ch-sp; rep from * to last 1ch-sp, 1ch, 1tr into last 1ch-sp, 1ch, skip 1 tr, 1tr into top of tch, turn.
Row 2 (RS): 3ch (counts as 1tr), 1tr into 1ch-sp, *1ch, 1tr into next 1ch-sp; rep from * to last 1ch-sp, 1ch, 1tr into last 1ch-sp, 1tr into third ch of tch, turn.
Repeat rows 1–2 until 46 rows have been completed.
Fasten off.

Lace edging

With right sides together, sew together the top edge of the last row of the Front and Back pieces. Using 2.5mm (US B1/C2) crochet hook and the right side facing, work 92dc along side edge of first crochet panel, 1dc into seam area, 92dc along side edge of remaining crochet panel, turn. (185 sts)

Row 1: 1ch, 1dc into each stitch to end of row, turn.
Rows 2, 3 AND 4: Repeat row 1.
Row 5: 3ch (counts as 1tr), skip st at base of beg-3ch, 1tr into each st to end of row, turn.
Row 6: 1ch, 1dc into each st to end of row, work final dc into top of tch, turn. (185 sts)
Rows 7, 8 AND 9: Repeat row 1.
Row 10: 4ch (counts as 1tr, 1ch), skip st at base of beg-4ch, 1tr into next st, *1ch, skip 1 st, 1tr into next st; repeat from * to last st, 1tr, turn.
Row 11: 3ch (counts as 1tr), skip 2 tr, 1tr into next 1ch-sp, *1ch, skip 1 tr, 1tr into next 1ch-sp; repeat from * to end of round, skip 1 tr, 1tr into top of tch, turn.
Row 12: 4ch (counts as 1tr, 1ch), skip 2 tr, 1tr into next 1ch-sp, *6ch, skip next 1ch-sp, 1tr into foll 1ch-sp, [1ch, 1tr into next 1ch-sp] twice; repeat from * 21 times more, 6ch, skip next 1ch-sp, 1tr into foll 1ch-sp, 1ch, 1tr into third ch of tch, turn.
Row 13: 1ch, ss into next 1ch-sp, ss into top of tr, *[2dc, 2htr, 5tr, 2htr, 2dc] into next 6ch-sp, [ss into top of tr, skip 1ch-sp] twice, ss into top of tr; repeat from * 21 times more, [2dc, 2htr, 5tr, 2htr, 2dc] into next 6ch-sp,

ss into top of tr, skip 1ch-sp, ss into top of tch, turn.

Row 14: 4ch, skip [2ss, 2dc and 2htr], *1tr into next tr, 3ch, skip 1 tr, dtr into next tr, 3ch, 1dtr into same sp as last tr, 3ch, skip 1 tr, 1tr into next tr, 3ch, skip [2htr, 2dc and 1ss], 1tr into next ss, 3ch, skip [1ss, 2dc and 2htr]; repeat from * 21 times, 1tr into next tr, 3ch, skip 1 tr, dtr into next tr, 3ch, 1dtr into same sp as last tr, 3ch, skip 1 tr, 1tr into next tr, 4ch, skip [2htr, 2dc and 1ss], 1dc into next ss, turn.

Row 15: 1ch, [3dc into next sp] twice, into the next space *[3dc, 3ch, 1ss into st at base of 3ch to make picot, 3dc], [3dc into next sp] twice; repeat from * to end of row, 1dc into base of tch at end of row. Fasten off.

Repeat along the opposite side edge.

Finishing

Pin out onto a padded surface and lightly block.

Join remaining side seam.

Weave in loose ends.

Using the photograph as reference, sew buttons into place, weave the ribbon through the treble stitches on row 5 of the lace edgings and tie the ends into a bow.

Simple shapes and clever accents in monochrome shades help create a Chanel-inspired décor.

Coco

At the age of 18, Gabrielle Chanel was forced to leave the care system. She struggled to find permanent work and so started performing in bars and clubs in Paris. Gabrielle's stage name was 'Coco', which Chanel later said came from the French word *cocotte*, meaning 'kept woman'. Although Chanel never married, she did have a string of affluent lovers, many of whom provided her with a comfortable if not luxurious lifestyle.

This elegant cushion celebrates the coquettish side of Chanel's early life. A restrained basketweave pattern sets the background for the flourish of the contrasting doily and corsage.

Size
Approximately 41cm (16in) square

Materials
Rowan Cashsoft 4ply
in cream,
4 x 50g (1¾oz) balls

Black buttons,
5 x 10mm (⅜in)
Vintage doily,
1 x 20cm (8in) diameter
Black flower corsage,
1 x 15cm (6in)
Button for the centre of corsage

Square cushion pad,
45cm (18in) square cushion pad

3.25mm (US 3) knitting needles
Knitter's sewing or tapestry needle

Tension
25 stitches and 42 rows to 10cm (4in) square over stocking stitch when using 3.25mm (US 3) knitting needles. Adjust the needle size to achieve the correct tension.

Front
Cast on 107 sts.
Row 1 (RS): Knit.
Row 2: *P3, k5; repeat from * to last st 3 sts, p3.
Row 3: *K3, p5; repeat from * to last 3 sts, k3.
Row 4: Repeat row 2.
Row 5: Knit.
Row 6: P3, k1, p3, *k5, p3; repeat from * to last 4 sts, k1, p3.
Row 7: K3, p1, *k3, p5; repeat from * to last 7 sts, k3, p1, k3.
Row 8: Repeat row 6.

Repeat rows 1–8 until the piece measures 41cm (16in) from cast-on edge ending with either row 4 or row 8.
Cast off.

Lower Back panel
With the RS facing, pick up and knit 107 sts along the cast-on edge of the Front piece.
Row 1 (WS): Purl.
Row 2 (RS): Knit.
Row 3: *P3, k5; repeat from * to last st 3 sts, p3.

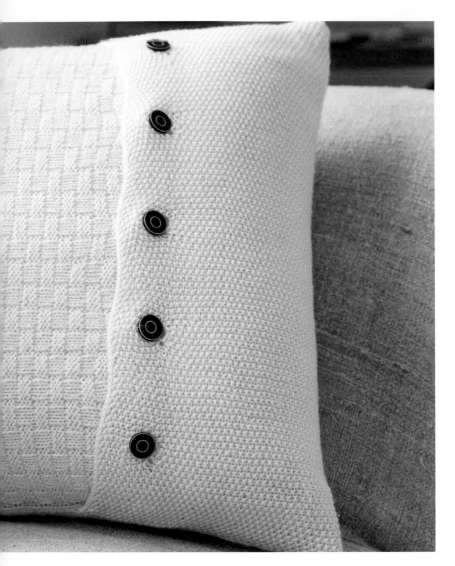

keeping stitch pattern correct as set and counting the st on the right-hand needle after the last buttonhole, work 15 sts; repeat from * to last st, k1. (5 buttonholes)

NEXT ROW (BUTTONHOLE CAST-ON ROW): Keeping stitch pattern correct as set work 16 sts, *turn, using the cable method and wrapping the final stitch, cast on 3 sts, turn, keeping stitch pattern correct as set work 15 sts; repeat from * to last st, k1. (107 sts) Continue in stitch pattern as set until piece measures 17cm (6¾in) from cast-on seam ending with RS row. Cast off.

Finishing

Pin out the Front and Back pieces onto a padded surface and lightly block.

Using mattress stitch, sew the side seams.

Weave loose ends into the seam stitches.

Secure buttons to the Lower Back panel in line with the buttonholes. To decorate, attach vintage crochet piece, black corsage and button.

Row 4: *K3, p5; repeat from * to last 3 sts, k3.
Row 5: Repeat row 3.
Row 6: Knit.
Row 7: P3, k1, p3, *k5, p3; repeat from * to last 4 sts, k1, p3.
Row 8: K3, p1, *k3, p5; repeat from * to last 7 sts, k3, p1, k3.
Row 9: Repeat row 7.
Repeat rows 2–9 until the piece measures 30cm (12in) from cast-on seam ending with either row 5 or row 9.
Cast off.

Upper Back panel

With the RS facing, pick up and knit 107 sts along the cast-off edge of the Front piece.
Set moss stitch as follows:
Row 1 (WS): K1, *p1, k1; repeat from * to end of row.
Row 2 (RS): Repeat row 1.
Repeat these two rows until piece measures 13cm (5⅛in) from cast-on edge, ending with a WS row.
NEXT ROW (BUTTONHOLE CAST-OFF ROW) (RS): Keeping stitch pattern correct as set work 16 sts, *cast off 3 sts,

Size
Approximately 40cm (16in) wide around the top edge; 10cm (4in) deep

Materials
Rowan Siena Cotton 4ply in cream,
1 x 50g (1¾oz) ball

Debbie Abrahams beads size 6 in clear (034),
1 x 500 bead pack

Black ribbon,
1m (3ft) x 7mm (¼in)

Small lampshade

2.5mm (US 1/0) crochet hook
Knitter's sewing or tapestry needle
Fine sewing needle and thread

Tension
28 sts and 11 rows to 10cm (4in) square when using a 2.5mm (US 1/0) crochet hook.
Adjust the hook size to achieve the correct tension.

Pigalle

In 1909, Chanel began an affair with Captain Arthur Edward Capel. Capel financed Chanel's first shop and she became a licensed hat maker in 1910. The couple travelled extensively and had a busy social life of parties and holidays. Much of their time was spent in Paris, however. Chanel's career began to bloom in 1912, when actress Gabrielle Dorziat modelled one of her hats in the play *Bel Ami*.

This flirty lampshade cover celebrates the racy spirit of Paris's bohemian life. The lacy crochet takes on a lingerie-style look, and the piece is embellished with a narrow black ribbon and iridescent beads.

FOUNDATION ROW: 115ch, skip 1 ch, 1dc into each ch to end, turn. (114 sts)

Row 1: 1ch, 1dc into each st to end, turn.

Row 2: 4ch (counts as 1dtr), skip st at base of beg-4ch, 1dtr into each st to end, turn.

Row 3: 1ch, 1dc into each st to end, working final st into top of tch, turn.

Row 4: 1ch, 1dc into each st to end, turn.

Row 5: 3ch (counts as 1tr), skip st at base of beg-3ch, 1tr into each next 3 sts, 1ch, *1tr into each next 7 sts, 1ch; repeat from * 14 times more, 1tr into each next 3 sts, tr2tog over next 2 sts, turn.

Row 6: 3ch (counts as 1tr), skip st at base of beg-3ch, 1tr into each next 3 sts, 3ch, skip 1ch, *1tr into each next 7 sts, 3ch, skip 1ch; repeat from * 14 times more, 1tr into each next 4 sts, turn.

Row 7: 3ch (counts as 1tr), skip st at base of beg-3ch, 1tr into next st, tr2tog over next 2 sts, 2ch, 1tr into ch-sp, 2ch, *tr2tog over next 2 sts, 1tr into each next 3 sts, tr2tog over next 2 sts, 2ch, 1tr into ch-sp, 2ch; repeat from * 14 times more, tr2tog over next 2 sts, 1tr into each next 2 sts, turn.

Row 8: 3ch (counts as 1tr), skip st at base of beg-3ch, tr2tog over next 2 sts, 2ch, [1tr, 3ch, 1tr] into next tr, 2ch, *tr2tog over next 2 sts, 1tr into next st, tr2tog over next 2 sts, 2ch, [1tr, 3ch, 1tr] into next tr, 2ch; repeat from * 14 times more, tr2tog over next sts, 1tr into final st, turn.

Row 9: 3ch (counts as 1tr) skip st at base of beg-3ch, 1tr into next st, 3ch, 1tr into next tr, 3ch, 1dc into next ch-sp, 3ch, 1tr into next tr, 3ch, *tr3tog over next 3 sts, 3ch, 1tr into next tr, 3ch, 1dc into next ch-sp, 3ch, 1tr into next tr, 3ch; repeat from * 14 times more, tr2tog over next 2 sts, turn.

Row 10: 6ch (counts as 1tr and 3ch), *1tr into next tr, 3ch, 1dc into next ch-sp, 5ch, 1dc into next ch-sp, 3ch, 1tr into next tr, 3ch, 1tr into next tr, 3ch; repeat from * 14 times more, 1tr into next tr, 3ch, 1dc into next ch-sp, 5ch, 1dc into next ch-sp, 3ch, 1tr into next tr, 3ch, tr2tog over next 2 sts, turn.

Row 11: 4ch (counts as 1tr and 1ch), *1tr into next tr, 3ch, 1dc into next ch-sp, 9tr into 5ch-sp, 1dc into next ch-sp, 3ch, 1tr into next tr, 3ch, skip 2 ch-sp; repeat from * 14 times more, 1tr into next tr, 3ch, 1dc into next ch-sp, 9tr into 5ch-sp, 1dc into

next ch-sp, 3ch, 1tr into next tr, 1ch, 1tr into top of tch.
Fasten off.

Finishing

Pin out onto a padded surface and lightly block.

Weave in loose ends.

Using a fine needle and sewing thread, sew groups of 10 beads to the central ch-sp between the groups of 9tr.

Mark the centre. Thread ribbon through the row of dtr from the centre to the side and then from the other edge back to the centre; place the lace edging around lampshade and tie a bow.

Make sure the opening sits at the back of the lamp.

Rivoli

Chanel sold a limited number of garments alongside her hat designs and won a dedicated clientele who made her practical sportswear range a great success. Chanel discarded corsets for women, designing a more streamlined look. Most of her designs were made from knitted jersey, a fabric traditionally used for men's undergarments. Chanel's choice of jersey was originally inspired by cost, although she continued using it long after her business became profitable.

This sophisticated-looking knitted cushion celebrates the streamlined look for which Chanel became renowned. The contrasting stripes give the piece a breezy, almost nautical look.

Size
Approximately 42cm (16½in) square

Materials
Rowan Cashsoft 4ply
in cream (A),
3 x 50g (1¾oz) balls
in black (B),
1 x 50g (1¾oz) ball

Debbie Abrahams beads size 6
in grey (606),
3 x 500 bead pack

Square cushion pad,
45cm (18in) square

3.25mm (US 3) knitting needles
Knitter's sewing or tapestry needle

Tension
26 stitches and 36 rows to 10cm (4in) square over stocking stitch when using 3.25mm (US 3) knitting needles. Adjust the needle size to achieve the correct tension.

Threading instructions
Thread beads onto yarn A but remember that more than one ball of yarn is used and some balls will be used for the back of the cushion.

Front
Using A, cast on 115 sts.
Row 1 (RS): Knit.
Row 2 (WS): Purl.
Row 3: Knit.
Pattern repeat as follows:
Row 4: Using yarn B, purl.
Row 5: Using yarn A, k2, *pb1, k1; repeat from * to last st, k1.
Row 6: Using yarn B, purl.
Row 7: Using yarn B, knit.
Row 8: Using the Fair Isle technique work as follows: p1B, *p1A, p1B; repeat from * to end.
Row 9: Using the Fair Isle technique work as follows: k1A, *k1B, k1A; repeat from * to end of row.
Row 10: Using yarn A, p2, *pb1, p1; repeat from * to last st, p1.
Rows 11–15: Using yarn A, work in stocking stitch, starting with a purl row.

The last 12 rows (rows 4–15) set the pattern repeat.
Work pattern repeat 10 more times, then work rows 1–10 once more.
Using A and beginning with a knit row, work 4 rows in stocking stitch.
Cast off.

Back
With the right side facing and using A, pick up and knit 115 sts along cast-on edge of the Front piece. Starting with a purl row, work 145 rows in stocking stitch.
Cast off.

Finishing
Pin out the Front and Back pieces onto a padded surface and lightly block.

Weave in loose ends.

Using A and mattress stitch, sew the Back and Front pieces together, inserting the cushion pad into the cover before completing the seam.

Fleur

Size
Approximately 42cm (16½in) square

Materials
Rowan Cotton Glace
in oyster,
7 x 50g (1¾oz) balls

Debbie Abrahams beads size 6
in black (748),
2 x 500 bead pack

Square cushion pad,
45cm (18in) square

3mm (US C-2) crochet hook
Knitter's sewing or tapestry needle

Tension
22 sts and 24–25 rows to 10cm
(4in) square over double crochet
when using a 3mm (US C-2) crochet
hook. Adjust the hook size to achieve
the correct tension.

By 1919 Chanel was registered as a couturier and had established her Maison de Couture at 31 rue Chambon in Paris. Women came to love Chanel's simple and comfortable styles with their boxy lines and shortened skirts that were both practical and elegant. Elements of these early designs featured in Chanel's collections for the rest of her career.

This elegant two-tone crochet cushion celebrates the spirit of Chanel. The stylized and regal-looking design, picked out in black beads, is set against a simple cream background.

Threading instructions

Thread beads onto yarn but remember that more than one ball of yarn is used and some balls will be used for the back of the cushion.

Front

FOUNDATION ROW: 94ch, skip 1 ch, 1dc into each ch to end, turn. (93 sts)

Row 1 (WS): 1ch, 1dc into each st to end, turn.

Repeat the last row 7 more times.

Row 9 (WS): 1ch, 1dc into each next 15 sts, work 63 sts from chart, working from left to right and placing beads as indicated, 1dc into last 15 sts, 1ch, turn.

Row 10 (RS): 1ch, 1dc into each next 15 sts, work 63 sts from chart, working from right to left, 1dc into last 15 sts, 1ch, turn.

Continue to work in pattern set, working from the chart across the centre 63 sts; placing beads and double crochet as indicated on WS rows and working RS rows in double crochet only.

Rows 96–104: 1ch, 1dc into each st to end, turn.

Fasten off.

Key

	oyster, dc
●	place bead, black

Back

FOUNDATION ROW: 94ch, skip 1 ch, 1dc into each ch to end, turn. (93 sts)

Row 1 (WS): 1ch, 1dc into each st to end, turn.

Repeat the last row until a total of 102 rows (including the foundation row) have been worked.

Fasten off.

Finishing

Pin out onto a padded surface and lightly block.

Weave in loose ends.

Join the Back and Front pieces together; with the wrong sides facing inwards, work double crochet stitches through the edge stitches of both pieces, inserting the cushion pad into the cover before completing the round.

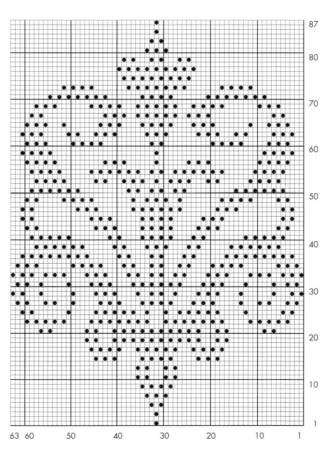

Time for Tea

At times of economic downturn it is common to see an upsurge in people looking to the craft market for ways of filling their spare time and learning new hobbies. Coupled with the awareness of our need to conserve our planet and educate future generations, there has been a massive trend towards the ethos of the 'make do and mend' era. Traditional crafts are making a speedy comeback and the vogue for all things vintage is abundantly reflected in current interior design, fashion and lifestyle choices. This design story was inspired by the interiors and lifestyle choices of the 1950s, 60s and 70s. It has a quirky vintage feel, with floral imagery, sugar-sweet and faded shades of yarn, embroidery stitches, crochet lace and cable stitches that are used to create pretty feminine pieces that pay homage to our 'crafty' past.

Angelica

Size
Approximately 38cm (15in) diameter

Materials
Rowan Wool Cotton
in light pink (MC),
3 x 50g (1¾oz) balls

Rowan Siena 4ply
in cream (CC),
1 x 50g (1¾oz) ball

Small amount of waste DK-weight yarn

Button, 1 large
Decorative braid,
120cm (48in) approximately
Round cushion pad,
40cm (16in) diameter

4mm (US 6) knitting needles
2.5mm (US 1/0) crochet hook
Knitter's sewing or tapestry needle

Tension
24 stitches and 30 rows to 10cm
(4in) square over stocking stitch when
using 4mm (US 6) knitting needles.
Adjust the needle size to achieve the
correct tension.

One crochet medallion measures
approximately 6cm (2⅜in) across the
diameter when using a 2.5mm
(US 1/0) crochet hook. Adjust the
crochet hook size to achieve the
correct tension.

'Make do and mend' was the ethos of the era of the two world wars, when money and materials were scarce and it was commonplace to mend clothes rather than buying brand new styles. Dressmaking and knitting were seen as necessary skills. At times of economic downturn, people often turn towards traditional crafts, both for the comfort and creativity that such crafts offer and to save money. A revival of craft skills often goes together with a rediscovery of vintage fashion and home furnishings and postwar trends are particularly treasured.

This pretty cushion celebrates the delicate pastel colours often found in postwar fashions. The body of the cushion is knitted, while the edge is trimmed with crochet and decorative braid. A vintage-style button sits at the centre.

Back and Front (both alike)

Using 4mm (US 6) knitting needles and waste yarn, cast on 35 sts.
Knit one row.
Break off waste yarn. Join in MC.
Row 1 (WS): Purl.
Row 2: K30, wrap the next stitch, turn.
Rows 3, 5, 7, 9, 11 and 13: Purl.
Row 4: K25, wrap the next stitch, turn.
Row 6: K20, wrap the next stitch, turn.
Row 8: K15, wrap the next stitch, turn.
Row 10: K10, wrap the next stitch, turn.
Row 12: K5, wrap the next stitch, turn.
Row 14 (RS): Knit across the row, moving the wrapped yarn to the WS by inserting the right-hand needle under the wrap, then into the wrapped stitch and knitting the two together.
Repeat rows 1–14, 23 times more. (24 pattern repeats)
Break off MC. Join in waste yarn.
Next row (WS): Purl.
Cast off.

Crochet medallion (make 2)

Foundation ring: Using 2.5mm (US 1/0) crochet hook and yarn (CC), 6ch, join with a ss to form a ring.
Round 1: 3ch (counts as 1tr), work 13tr into ring, ss to join to top of beg-3ch. (14 sts)
Round 2: 3ch (counts as 1tr), 1tr into st at base of beg-3ch, 2tr into each st to end of round, ss to join to top of beg-3ch. (28 sts)
Round 3: 3ch (counts as 1tr), skip st at base of beg-3ch, *2tr into next st, 1tr into next st; repeat from * to final st, 2tr into next st, ss to join to top of beg-3ch. (42 sts)
Fasten off.

Crochet edging

Foundation ring: Using 2.5mm (US 1/0) crochet hook and yarn (CC), 288ch, making sure ch is not twisted, join with a ss to form a ring.
Round 1: 1ch, 1dc into each ch to end of round, ss to join to top of beg-1ch.
Round 2: 1ch, 1dc into next st, *2ch, skip 2 sts, 1dc into next st; repeat from * to end of round, 2ch, skip 2 sts, ss to join to top of beg-1ch.

Round 3: Ss into next 1ch-sp, 4ch (counts as 1tr, 1ch), [1tr, 1ch, 1tr] into same 1ch-sp, skip 2 dc, *[1tr, 1ch, 1tr, 1ch, 1tr] into next 1ch-sp; repeat from * to end of round, ss to join to third ch of beg-4ch.
Round 4: *3ch (counts as 1tr), 1tr into 1ch-sp at base of 3ch, 2tr into next 1ch-sp, ss into next 1ch-sp; repeat from * to end of round.
Fasten off.

Finishing

Complete the Back piece by threading MC into a knitter's needle or tapestry needle and grafting the first row of MC knitting to the last row of MC knitting to create an invisible seam. Unravel the waste yarn. Repeat for the Front piece.

Reduce the hole in the centre of the Back piece by using MC and running stitch to sew around the edge of the open hole at the centre of the Back piece. Gently gather the edge, leaving a small hole at the centre. Secure the end. Repeat for the Front piece.

Pin out the Back and Front pieces onto a padded surface and block. Attach a crochet medallion in the centre of the Back and Front pieces. Secure the button in the centre of the crochet medallion on the Front piece. Weave in loose ends.

Using MC and mattress stitch, sew the Back and Front pieces together, inserting the cushion pad into the cover before completing the seam. Lightly block the crochet edging. Pin the crochet edging around the outside edge of the cushion, easing it in to fit evenly around the cushion. Sew the crochet edging in place. Pin and sew the decorative braid around the edge of the cushion.

Madeleine

During the world wars women were often recruited into the workplace as replacement labour while men were away. After the wars, it was more acceptable for women to take jobs, although many still adhered to the 'ideal' female role of housekeeping and raising a family. The 1950s saw a rise in incomes, while the introduction of appliances such as washing machines and gas cookers meant that many domestic tasks took less time. These advances helped increase leisure time and many women turned to traditional crafts not so much out of necessity but as a means of beautifying their homes.

This elegant cushion celebrates the aesthetic of this era. Knitted tucks radiate out from the centre, while the edging features a dense cable pattern. For an authentic nod to vintage style, embellish the centre of the cushion with a co-ordinating button.

Size

Approximately 45cm (18in) diameter

Materials

Rowan Wool Cotton
in dark pink (MC),
7 x 50g (1¾oz) balls

Small amount of waste DK-weight yarn

Buttons, 2 large
Round cushion pad,
50cm (20in) diameter

4mm (US 6) knitting needles
2.5mm (US 1/0) knitting needle
One cable needle
Knitter's sewing or tapestry needle
Optional: loop stitch marker

Tension

22 stitches and 30 rows to 10cm (4in) square over stocking stitch when using 4mm (US 6) knitting needles. Adjust the needle size to achieve the correct tension.

Special abbreviations

Work a tuck row: With all stitches remaining on the knitting needle and the WS facing and starting at the left-hand side of the knitted piece, use the single 2.25mm (US 1/0) knitting needle to pick up the loop of each stitch of the row with a marker 4 rows down. (35 sts)

In the left hand, hold the 4mm (US 6) knitting needle (that holds the stitches just worked) behind and in line with the smaller needle (that holds the picked-up stitches) with the points of both needles pointing towards the right – as if waiting to be worked.

With the right hand, insert the 4mm (US 6) knitting needle purlwise into the next stitch on the back needle, then purlwise into the next stitch on the smaller needle. Purl these two stitches together. Continue to work along both needles, working two stitches together (one from each needle) to the end of the row to create a tuck.

C6B (cable 6 back): slip 3 stitches purlwise to cable needle and hold at the back of the work, k3 from the left-hand needle, k3 from cable needle.

C6F (cable 6 front): slip 3 stitches purlwise to cable needle and hold at the front of the work, k3 from the left-hand needle, k3 from cable needle.

Row 10: K20, wrap the next stitch, turn.

Row 12: K15, wrap the next stitch, turn.

Row 14: K10, wrap the next stitch, turn.

Row 16: K5, wrap the next stitch, turn.

Row 17: Purl, mark the beginning of this row with a short length of waste yarn or a stitch marker.

Row 18 (RS): Knit across the row, moving the wrapped yarn to the WS by inserting the right-hand needle under the wrap, then into the wrapped stitch and knitting the two together.

Repeat rows 1–18, 23 times more. (24 pattern repeats)

Break off MC. Join in waste yarn.

Next row (WS): Purl.

Cast off.

Cable panels (make 2)

Using 4mm (US 6) knitting needles and waste yarn, cast on 26 sts.

Knit one row.

Purl one row.

Break off waste yarn. Join in MC.

Row 1 (RS): Knit.

Row 2: Purl.

Row 3: K4, *C6B; repeat from * to last 4 sts, k4.

Row 4: Purl.

Row 5: Knit.

Row 6: Purl.

Row 7: K1, *C6F; repeat from * to last st, k1.

Row 8: Purl.

Repeat rows 1–8, 4 times more. (5 pattern repeats)

Repeat rows 1–7, once more.

Break off MC. Join in waste yarn.

Next row (WS): Purl.

Cast off.

Back and Front (both alike)

Using 4mm (US 6) knitting needles and waste yarn, cast on 35 sts.

Knit one row.

Break off waste yarn. Join in MC.

Row 1 (WS): Purl, mark the beginning of this row with a short length of waste yarn or a stitch marker.

Row 2: Knit.

Row 3: Purl.

Row 4: Knit.

Row 5: Work a tuck row.

Row 6: K30, wrap the next stitch, turn.

Rows 7, 9, 11, 13, 15 and 17: Purl.

Row 8: K25, wrap the next stitch, turn.

Finishing

Complete the Back piece by threading MC into a knitter's needle or tapestry needle and grafting the first row of MC knitting to the last row of MC knitting to create an invisible seam. Unravel the waste yarn. Repeat for the Front piece.

Reduce the hole in the centre of the Back piece by using MC and running stitch to sew around the edge of the open hole at the centre of the Back piece. Gently gather the edge, leaving a small hole at the centre. Secure the end. Repeat for the Front piece.

Pin out the Back and Front pieces onto a padded surface and lightly block.

Join a Cable panel piece by using MC and the same technique as for the Back and Front pieces; graft the first row of MC knitting to the last row of MC knitting to create knitted loops. Repeat for the other Cable panel piece.

Using MC and mattress stitch, sew one cable panel to the outside edge of the Back piece, easing the tuck areas as required. Repeat for the Front piece.

Weave loose ends into the seam stitches.

Using MC and mattress stitch, sew the Back and Front pieces together, inserting the cushion pad into the cover before completing the seam.

Secure a large button in the centre of both the Back and Front pieces, sewing through the centre of the cushion pad in order to create a 'deep button' effect.

Size
Approximately 25cm (10in) diameter

Materials
Rowan Siena 4ply
in light pink or dark pink
1 x 50g (1¾oz) ball

2.5mm (US B-1) crochet hook
Knitter's sewing or tapestry needle

Tension
One doily measures approximately
25cm (10in) across the diameter
when using a 2.5mm (US B-1)
crochet hook. Adjust the crochet hook
size to achieve the correct tension.

Victoria

Crochet was popular during the Victorian era; Queen Victoria herself was photographed with yarn and hook in hand. During the time of the two world wars crochet went into something of a decline, while knitting enjoyed increased popularity. This may have been as a result of rationing and the difficulty in sourcing yarns, however, the 1950s to 1970s saw a revival in crochet, with lacy patterns and doily work proving very popular.

These doilies, worked in pale pink cotton, celebrate the delicacy of crochet work, which replicates the look of lace so well (in Victorian times crochet had been called 'poor man's lace'). They make the perfect table decoration for a genteel tea time.

FOUNDATION RING: 6ch, join with a ss to form a ring.

ROUND 1: 3ch (counts as 1tr), 11tr into centre of ring, ss to join to top of beg-3ch. (12 sts)

ROUND 2: 3ch (counts as 1tr), 1tr into st at base of beg-3ch, *2tr into next st; repeat from * to end of round, ss to join to top of beg-3ch. (24 sts)

ROUND 3: 3ch (counts as 1tr), skip st at base of beg-3ch, 2tr into next st, *1tr into next st, 2tr into next st; repeat from * to end of round, ss to join to top of beg-3ch. (36 sts)

ROUND 4: 4ch (counts as 1tr, 1ch), 1tr into st at base of beg-4ch, 1ch, *skip 1 st, 1tr into next st, 1ch, 1tr into same st, 1ch; repeat from * to end of round, ss to join to third ch of beg-4ch.

ROUND 5: Ss into next ch-sp, 4ch (counts as 1tr, 1ch), [1tr, 1ch, 1tr] into same 1ch-sp, skip 1ch-sp, *[1tr, 1ch, 1tr, 1ch, 1tr] into next 1ch-sp; repeat from * to end of round, ss to join to third ch of beg-4ch.

ROUND 6: Ss into next 1ch-sp, *3ch (counts as 1tr), 1tr into 1ch-sp at base of beg-3ch, 2tr into next 1ch-sp, ss into next 1ch-sp; repeat from * to end of round, ss to join to first ch-sp at beg of round. (18 points)

ROUND 7: Ss into each of next 3 ch, 5ch, *1dc into top of next 'point', 5ch; repeat from * to end of round, ss to join to first ch of beg-5ch.

ROUND 8: Ss into next ch-sp, 4ch (counts as 1tr, 1ch), working into 5ch-sp at base of beg-4ch work [1tr, 1ch] 4 times, *working into next 5ch-sp, work [1tr, 1ch] 5 times; repeat from * to end of round, ss to join to third ch of beg-4ch.

ROUND 9: Ss into ch-sp, 3ch (counts as 1tr), 1tr into ch-sp at base of beg-3ch, 1tr into each next 2 1ch-sps, 2tr into next 1ch-sp, 1ch *2tr into next 1ch-sp, 1tr into each next 2 1ch-sps, 2tr into next 1ch-sp, 1ch; repeat from * to end of round, ss to join to top of beg-3ch.

ROUND 10: Ss into st-sp between 2tr, 3ch (counts as 1tr), 1tr into st-sp at base of beg-3ch, 1tr into next 3 st-sps, 2tr into st-sp between next 2tr, 1ch, *skip 1 ch, 2tr into st-sp between next 2tr, 1tr into next 3 st-sps, 2tr into st-sp between next 2tr, 1ch; repeat from * to end of round, ss to join to top of beg-3ch.

ROUND 11: Ss into st-sp between 2tr, 3ch (counts as 1tr), skip 1 tr, 1tr into next 3 st-sps, working into st-sps made by next tr and the centre of tr2tog on previous round work tr2tog, 2ch, skip 1ch-sp, *1tr into next 4 st-sps, working into st-sps made by next tr and the centre of tr2tog on previous round work tr2tog, 2ch, skip 1ch-sp; repeat from * to end of round, ss to join to top of beg-3ch.

ROUND 12: Ss into st-sp between 2tr, 3ch (counts as 1tr), 1tr into next 2 st-sps, working into st-sps made by next tr and the centre of tr2tog on previous round work tr2tog, 5ch, skip 2ch-sp, *1tr into next 3 st-sps, working into st-sps made by next tr and the centre of tr2tog on previous round work tr2tog, 5ch, skip 2ch-sp; repeat from * to end of round, ss to join to top of beg-3ch.

ROUND 13: Ss into st-sp between 2tr, 3ch (counts as 1tr), working into next 2 st-sps tr2tog, 3ch, 1tr into 5ch-sp, 3ch, 1tr into same 5ch-sp, 3ch, *working into next 3 st-sps tr3tog, 3ch, 1tr into 5ch-sp, 3ch, 1tr into same 5ch-sp, 3ch; repeat from * to end of round, ss to join to top of beg-3ch.
Fasten off.

Finishing

Weave in loose ends.

Gently pin out the doily onto a padded surface and lightly block.

Size
Approximately 28cm (11in) square

Materials
Rowan Siena 4ply
in sage green (MC),
4 x 50g (1¾oz) balls

Small amounts of contrast 4ply
wool for embroidery,
Dark pink
Light pink
Red
Bright green
Dark green
Cream
Yellow
Duck egg blue

Square cushion pad,
30cm (12in) square

2.5mm (US B-1) crochet hook
Knitter's sewing or tapestry needle

Tension
23–24 sts and 26–27 rows to 10cm
(4in) square over double crochet
when using a 2.5mm (US B-1)
crochet hook. Adjust the hook size to
achieve the correct tension.

Madeira

In the early part of the 20th century women's fashion had seen a major shift in emphasis; designers such as Paul Poiret and Coco Chanel had redefined the shape of clothes and dispensed with corsets, girdles and complicated undergarments. However, after World War II women's fashions once again took on a more explicitly feminine and constructed look. The androgynous look of flapper dresses and unfitted sportswear was replaced by full skirts, nipped-in waists and accentuated bosoms. Fabrics were printed with pretty floral patterns and stitch detail and lace played an important part in the trend typified by Christian Dior's 'New Look'.

This refined-looking cushion is inspired by such feminine details. The colours are muted and harmonious and the design features a traditional floral motif worked in cross stitch on a crochet backdrop.

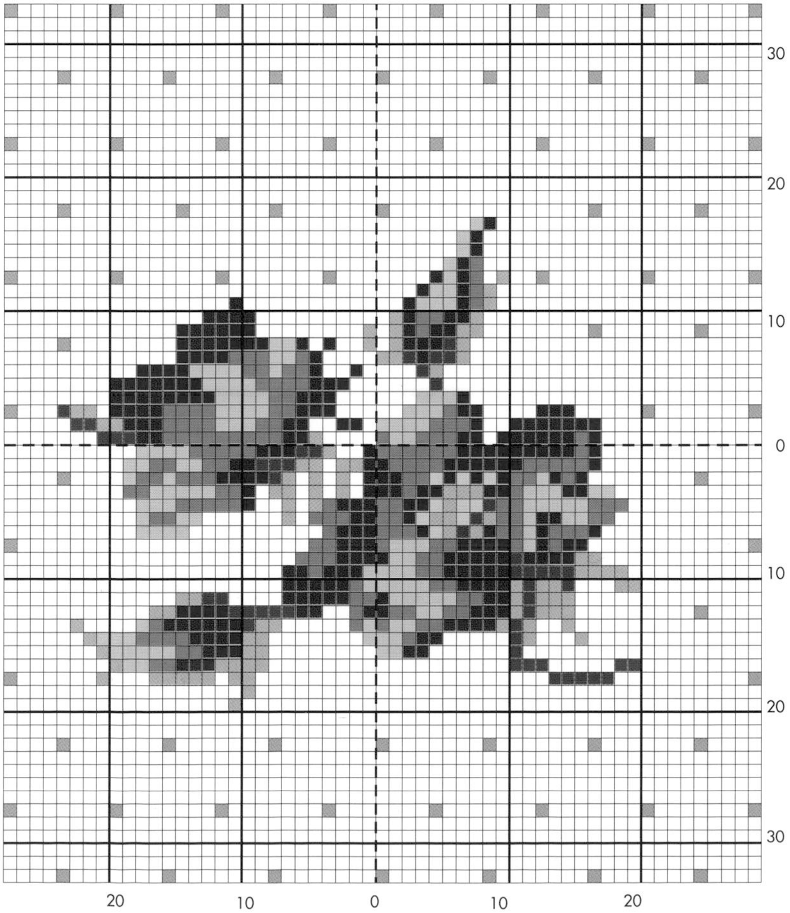

Back and Front (both alike)

FOUNDATION ROW: Using MC, 68ch, skip 1ch, 1dc into each ch to end, turn. (67 sts)

ROW 1: 1ch, 1dc into each st to end, turn.

Repeat row 1 until piece measures 28cm (11in) from foundation-chain edge.

Fasten off.

Finishing

Pin out the Front and Back pieces onto a padded surface and lightly block.

Weave in loose ends.

Mark the centre of the Front piece, then working from the chart, work the motif in cross stitch.

Using MC, join the Back and Front pieces together, with the wrong sides facing inwards. Work double crochet stitches evenly through both edges, inserting the cushion pad into the cover before completing the round.

Key

☐ sage green (MC), dc
■ dark pink, cross stitch
■ light pink, cross stitch
■ red, cross stitch
■ bright green, cross stitch
■ dark green, cross stitch
■ cream, cross stitch
■ yellow, cross stitch
■ duck egg blue, cross stitch

Florentine

The mid-20th century saw a massive shift in popular culture. Attitudes towards what was socially acceptable were changing; discussion of sexuality became more common, and music and film especially reflected the changes in what was considered decent. Rock 'n' roll emerged in the mid-1950s; lyrics were teen-focused and groups were fronted by 'edgy' young stars pushing the boundaries of respectability. Not everything changed, however; although more young women went into higher education and it was possible for women to have careers, the traditional paths of marriage and motherhood still beckoned.

This appealing cushion reflects the demure femininity that was still current in the 1950s. Crochet flowers in restrained colours are set against a beige knitted background. The addition of a ribbon sets off the posy.

Size
Approximately 38cm (15in) square

Materials
Rowan Revive
in light brown (MC),
3 x 50g (1¾oz) balls

Small amounts of contrast 4ply yarn
for flowers and leaves,
Red (A)
Pink (B)
Light pink (C)
Dark green (D)
Bright green (E)

Blue ribbon,
1m (3ft) x 7mm (¼in)
Buttons,
7 x 15mm (⅝in)
Square cushion pad,
40cm (16in) square

3.75mm (US 5) knitting needles
3mm (US C-2) crochet hook
Knitter's sewing or tapestry needle
Sewing needle and thread

Tension
23 stitches and 32 rows to 10cm (4in) square over stocking stitch when using 3.75mm (US 5) knitting needles. Adjust the needle size to achieve the correct tension.

Front and Back (both alike)

Using 3.75mm (US 5) knitting needles, cast on 38 sts.

Row 1 (RS): Knit.

Row 2: Purl.

These 2 rows set stocking stitch. Work in stocking stitch until piece measures 38cm (15in) ending with RS row.

Cast off.

Flower (make 7 using different colour combinations)

FOUNDATION RING: Using 3mm (US C-2) crochet hook and either A, B or C, 8ch, join with a ss to form a ring.

ROUND 1: 1ch, 15dc into centre of ring, ss to join to first dc.

ROUND 2: 5ch, skip st at base of beg-5ch and foll 2 sts, [ss into next st, 5ch, skip 2 sts] 4 times, ss to join to first ch of beg-5ch. (5ch-sp)

ROUND 3: 1ss into next ch-sp, *[1dc, 1htr, 5tr, 1htr, 1dc] into next ch-sp; repeat from * 4 times more, ss to join to first ch-sp. (5 petals) Fasten off.

Using a second colour from either A, B or C, join yarn to back of flower at the point between 2 petals.

ROUND 4: *8ch, ss into ss between the next 2 petals; repeat from * 3 times more, ss to join to first ss.

ROUND 5: 1ss into next ch-sp, *[1dc, 1htr, 8tr, 1htr, 1dc] into next ch-sp; repeat from * 4 times more, ss to join to first ch-sp. (5 petals)

Leaves (make 6)

FOUNDATION CHAIN: Using 3mm (US C-2) crochet hook and D, 20ch.

ROUND 1: Skip 2 ch, 1dc into each next 2 ch, 1htr into next ch, 1tr into each next 2 ch, 1dtr into each next 2 ch, dtr2tog over next 2 sts, 1dtr into next ch, 1tr into each next 2 ch, 1htr into next ch, ss into each next 5ch. Fasten off.

Repeat once more using D.

Repeat 4 times more using E.

Finishing

Pin out the Front and Back pieces onto a padded surface and lightly block.

Weave in loose ends.

Using the photograph as reference, sew crochet pieces in place.

Using D and E, embroider chain stitch to represent the flower stalks.

Tie a bow in the ribbon and stitch in place.

Attach buttons in the centre of the flowers.

Using MC and mattress stitch, sew the Back and Front pieces together, inserting the cushion pad into the cover before completing the seam.

Chelsea

Size
Approximately 62cm (24½in) diameter

Materials
Rowan Cotton Glace
in yellow (A),
1 x 50g (1¾oz) ball
in pink (B),
1 x 50g (1¾oz) ball
in red (C),
1 x 50g (1¾oz) ball
in bright green (D),
1 x 50g (1¾oz) ball
in olive green (E),
1 x 50g (1¾oz) ball

2.5mm (US 1/0) crochet hook
Knitter's sewing or tapestry needle

Tension
The first 3 rounds measure
approximately 10cm (4in) across
the diameter when using a 2.5mm
(US 1/0) crochet hook. Adjust the
crochet hook size to achieve the
correct tension.

By the 1960s, the place of women in society had changed quite
dramatically. It was more common for women to enjoy full
education and seek a professional career. Fashions changed
dramatically; skirts became significantly shorter and the
androgynous, elfin look was promoted once again by fashion
designers such as Mary Quant. However, despite the notion of
'free love' and all that went with it, women were still encouraged
to seek romantic ideals and were still primarily responsible for
providing a stable and loving home life for their family.

This oversized crochet doily, large enough to decorate a small
table, celebrates the free-spiritedness of the 1960s with its
vibrant colours.

Doily
FOUNDATION RING: Using A, 9ch, join
with a ss to form a ring.
ROUND 1: 3ch (counts as first step of
cluster), tr2tog into ring, 4ch, *tr3tog
into ring, 4ch; rep from * 7 times
more, ss into top of beg-3ch, ss into
ch-sp joining in B.
ROUND 2: 3ch (counts as first step of
cluster), tr2tog into same ch-sp, 3ch,
tr3tog into same ch-sp, 3ch,
*[tr3tog, 3ch, tr3tog] into next
ch-sp, 3ch; rep from * to end of
round, ss into top of tr2tog (cluster) at
beg of round.
ROUND 3: 3ch (counts as first step of
cluster), tr2tog into base of beg-3ch
to form cluster, 3ch, tr3tog into next
ch-sp, 3ch, tr3tog into top of next
cluster on previous row, 3ch, *tr3tog
into top of next cluster, 3ch, tr3tog
into next ch-sp, 3ch, tr3tog into top
of cluster, 3ch; rep from * to end of

round, ss into top of tr2tog (cluster) at
beg of round, joining in C.
ROUND 4: 3ch (counts as first step of
cluster), tr2tog into base of beg-3ch
to form cluster, 3ch, skip next ch-sp,
[tr3tog, 3ch, tr3tog] into top of next
cluster, 3ch, *[skip next ch-sp, tr3tog
into top of next cluster, 3ch] twice,
skip next ch-sp, [tr3tog, 3ch, tr3tog]
into top of next cluster, 3ch; rep from
* to last cluster, skip next ch-sp, tr3tog
into top of next cluster, 3ch, ss into
top of tr2tog (cluster) at beg of round.
ROUND 5: 3ch (counts as first step of
cluster), tr2tog into base of beg-3ch
to form cluster, 3ch, skip next ch-sp,
tr3tog into top of next cluster, 3ch,
tr3tog into next ch-sp, 3ch, tr3tog
into top of next cluster, 3ch, skip next
ch-sp, tr3tog into top of next cluster,
3ch, skip next ch-sp, *tr3tog into top
of next cluster, 3ch, skip next ch-sp,
tr3tog into top of next cluster, 3ch,

tr3tog into next ch-sp, 3ch, tr3tog into top of next cluster, 3ch, skip next ch-sp, tr3tog into top of next cluster, 3ch, skip next ch-sp; rep from * to end of round, ss into top of tr2tog (cluster) at beg of round.

Round 6: 3ch (counts as first step of cluster), tr2tog into base of beg-3ch to form cluster, 3ch, skip next ch-sp, [tr3tog into top of next cluster, 3ch, skip next ch-sp] 3 times, tr3tog into top of next cluster, 5ch, skip next ch-sp, *[tr3tog into top of next cluster, 3ch, skip next ch-sp] 4 times, tr3tog into top of next cluster, 5ch, skip next ch-sp; rep from * to end of round, ss into top of tr2tog (cluster) at beg of round.

Round 7: 3ch (counts as first step of cluster), tr2tog into base of beg-3ch to form cluster, 3ch, skip next ch-sp, [tr3tog into top of next cluster, 3ch, skip next ch-sp] 3 times, tr3tog into top of next cluster, 9ch, skip next ch-sp, *[tr3tog into top of next cluster, 3ch, skip next ch-sp] 4 times, tr3tog into top of next cluster, 9ch, skip next ch-sp; rep from * to end of round, ss into top of tr2tog (cluster) at beg of round.

Round 8: 3ch (counts as first step of cluster), tr2tog into base of beg-3ch to form cluster, 3ch, skip next ch-sp, [tr3tog into top of next cluster, 1ch, skip next ch-sp] twice, tr3tog into top of next cluster, 3ch, tr3tog into top of next cluster, 5ch, dc into 9ch-sp on previous round, 5ch, *tr3tog into top of next cluster, 3ch, skip next ch-sp, [tr3tog into top of next cluster, 1ch, skip next ch-sp] twice, tr3tog into top of next cluster, 3ch, tr3tog into top of next cluster, 5ch, dc into 9ch-sp on previous round, 5ch; rep from * to end of round, ss into top of tr2tog (cluster) at beg of round.

Round 9: 3ch (counts as first step of cluster), tr2tog into base of beg-3ch to form cluster, 3ch, skip next ch-sp, tr3tog into top of next cluster, 1ch, skip [1ch, 1cluster, 1ch], tr3tog into top of next cluster, 3ch, tr3tog into top of next cluster, 6ch, 1tr into dc on previous round, 7ch, 1tr into same st, 6ch, *tr3tog into top of next cluster, 3ch, skip next ch-sp, tr3tog into top of next cluster, 1ch, skip [1ch, 1cluster, 1ch], tr3tog into top of next cluster, 3ch, tr3tog into top of next cluster, 6ch, 1tr into dc on previous round, 7ch, 1tr into same st, 6ch; rep from * to end of round, ss into top of tr2tog (cluster) at beg of round.

Round 10: 3ch (counts as first step of cluster), tr2tog into base of beg-3ch to form cluster, 1ch, skip next ch-sp and next cluster, tr3tog into next ch-sp, 1ch, skip next cluster and next ch-sp, tr3tog into top of next cluster, 7ch, 1tr into top of tr on previous round, 7ch, 1tr into next ch-sp, 7ch, 1tr into top of next tr, 7ch, skip next ch-sp, *tr3tog into top of next cluster, 1ch, skip next ch-sp and next cluster, tr3tog into next ch-sp, 1ch, skip next cluster and next ch-sp, tr3tog into top of next cluster, 7ch, 1tr into top of tr on previous round, 7ch, 1tr into next ch-sp, 7ch, 1tr into top of next tr on previous round, 7ch, skip next ch-sp; rep from * to end of round, ss into top of tr2tog (cluster) at beg of round.

Round 11: 3ch (counts as first step of cluster), tr2tog into base of beg-3ch to form cluster, 1ch, skip next ch-sp, next cluster and next ch-sp, tr3tog into top of next cluster, 7ch, 1tr into top of tr on previous round, 7ch, 1tr into top of next tr on previous round, 5ch, 1tr into same st, 7ch, 1tr into

top of next tr, 7ch, skip next ch-sp, *tr3tog into top of next cluster, 1ch, skip next ch-sp, next cluster and next ch-sp, tr3tog into top of next cluster, 7ch, 1tr into top of tr on previous round, 7ch, 1tr into top of next tr on previous round, 5ch, 1tr into same st, 7ch, 1tr into top of next tr, 7ch, skip next ch-sp; rep from * to end of round, ss into top of tr2tog (cluster) at beg of round.

Round 12: 3ch (counts as first step of cluster), tr2tog into base of beg-3ch to form cluster, 9ch, skip next ch-sp, 1dc into top of next tr, 9ch, skip next ch-sp, 1dc into 5ch-sp on previous round, 9ch, skip next ch-sp, 1dc into top of next tr, 9ch, skip next ch-sp, *tr3tog into top of next cluster, 9ch, skip next ch-sp, 1dc into top of next tr, 9ch, skip next ch-sp, 1dc into 5ch-sp on previous round, 9ch, skip next ch-sp, 1dc into top of next tr, 9ch, skip next ch-sp; rep from * to end of round, ss into top of tr2tog (cluster) at beg of round, joining in D.

Round 13: 4ch (counts as first step of cluster), dtr2tog into st at base of 4ch to form cluster, 5ch, 1dc into next ch-sp, 5ch, dtr2tog into next dc, 5ch, 1dc into next ch-sp, 5ch, dtr3tog into next dc, 5ch, 1dc into next ch-sp, 5ch, dtr2tog into next dc, 5ch, 1dc into next ch-sp, 5ch, *dtr3tog into next dc, 5ch, dtr2tog into next dc, 5ch, 1dc into next ch-sp, 5ch, dtr3tog into next dc, 5ch, 1dc into next ch-sp, 5ch, dtr2tog into next dc, 5ch, 1dc into next ch-sp, 5ch; rep from * to end of round, ss into top of dtr2tog (cluster) at beg of round.

Round 14: 4ch (counts as first step of cluster), dtr2tog into st at base of 4ch to form cluster, 5ch, [dtr3tog, 2ch, dtr2tog, 3ch, dtr3tog] into top of next cluster, 5ch, *dtr3tog into top of next cluster, 5ch, [dtr3tog, 2ch, dtr2tog, 3ch, dtr3tog] into top of next cluster, 5ch; rep from * to end of round, ss into top of dtr2tog (cluster) at beg of round.

ROUND 15: 4ch (counts as first step of cluster), dtr2tog into st at base of 4ch to form cluster, 2ch, dtr3tog into same st, 5ch, skip next ch-sp, dtr3tog into top of next cluster, 3ch, skip ch-sp, 5dtr into top of dtr2tog, 3ch, skip next ch-sp, dtr3tog into top of next cluster, 5ch, skip next ch-sp, *dtr3tog into top of next cluster, 2ch, dtr3tog into same st, 5ch, skip next ch-sp, dtr3tog into top of next cluster, 3ch, skip ch-sp, 5dtr into top of dtr2tog, 3ch, skip next ch-sp, dtr3tog into top of next cluster, 5ch, skip next ch-sp; rep from * to end of round, ss into top of dtr2tog (cluster) at beg of round.

ROUND 16: 4ch (counts as first step of cluster), dtr2tog into st at base of 4ch to form cluster, 4ch, 1dtr into next ch-sp, 4ch, dtr3tog into top of next cluster, 7ch, skip [next ch-sp, cluster and next ch-sp], 1dc into each next 5dtr on previous round, 7ch, skip [next ch-sp, cluster and next ch-sp], *dtr3tog into top of next cluster, 4ch, 1dtr into next ch sp, 4ch, dtr3tog into top of next cluster, 7ch, skip [next ch-sp, cluster and next ch-sp], 1dc into each next 5dtr on previous round, 7ch, skip [next ch-sp, cluster and next ch-sp]; rep from * to end of round, ss into top of dtr2tog (cluster) at beg of round, ss into ch-sp joining in E.

ROUND 17: 4ch (counts as first step of cluster), dtr2tog into st at base of 4ch to form cluster, 6ch, 1dtr into top of dtr on previous round, 6ch, dtr3tog into top of next cluster, 7ch, skip next ch-sp, dtr5tog over next 5dc, 7ch,

skip next ch-sp, *dtr3tog into top of next cluster, 6ch, 1dtr into top of dtr on previous round, 6ch, dtr3tog into top of next cluster, 7ch, skip next ch-sp, dtr5tog over next 5dc, 7ch, skip next ch-sp; rep from * to end of round, ss into top of dtr2tog (cluster) at beg of round.

ROUND 18: 4ch (counts as first step of cluster), dtr2tog into st at base of 4ch to form cluster, 7ch, 1dtr into top of dtr on previous round, 3ch, 1dtr into same st, 7ch, skip next ch-sp, dtr3tog into top of next cluster, 6ch, skip next ch-sp, 1dc into top of dtr5tog, 6ch, skip next ch-sp, *dtr3tog into top of next cluster, 7ch, 1dtr into top of dtr on previous round, 3ch, 1dtr into same st, 7ch, skip next ch-sp, dtr3tog into top of next cluster, 6ch, skip next ch-sp, 1dc into top of dtr5tog, 6ch, skip next ch-sp; rep from * to end of round, ss into top of dtr2tog (cluster) at beg of round.

ROUND 19: 4ch (counts as first step of cluster), dtr2tog into st at base of 4ch to form cluster, 9ch, 3dtr into top of next dtr on previous round, into next ch-sp, [2ch, 1dtr] twice, 2ch, 3dtr into top of next dtr on previous round, 9ch, skip next ch-sp, 3dtr into top of next cluster, 6ch, skip next ch-sp, 1dc into next dc, 6ch, skip next ch-sp, *dtr3tog into top of next cluster, 9ch, 3dtr into top of next dtr on previous round, into next ch-sp, [2ch, 1dtr] twice, 2ch, 3dtr into top of next dtr on previous round, 9ch, skip next ch-sp, 3dtr into top of next cluster, 6ch, skip next ch-sp, 1dc into next dc, 6ch, skip next ch-sp; rep from * to end of round, ss into top of dtr2tog (cluster) at beg of round.

ROUND 20: 4ch (counts as first step of cluster), dtr2tog into st at base of 4ch to form cluster, 8ch, skip next ch-sp,

dtr3tog over next 3sts, 6ch, skip next ch-sp, dtr5tog into next ch-sp, 4ch, ss into first ch, [3ch, ss into same ch] twice to form picot, 6ch, skip next ch-sp, dtr3tog over next 3sts, 8ch, skip next ch-sp, dtr3tog into top of next cluster, 1ch, skip [next ch-sp, dc and next ch-sp], *dtr3tog into top of next cluster, 8ch, skip next ch-sp, dtr3tog over next 3sts, 6ch, skip next ch-sp, dtr5tog into next ch-sp, 4ch, ss into first ch, [3ch, ss into same ch] twice to form picot, 6ch, skip next ch-sp, dtr3tog over next 3sts, 8ch, skip next ch-sp, dtr3tog into top of next cluster, 1ch, skip [next ch-sp, dc and next ch-sp]; rep from * to end of round, ss into top of dtr2tog (cluster) at beg of round.
Fasten off.

Finishing

Weave in loose ends.

Gently pin out the doily onto a padded surface and lightly block.

Complement the colourful doily tablecloth with a pretty tea set.

Amandine

The three decades after World War II saw a demise in the extended family and the rise of the nuclear family. Older family members no longer lived alongside younger members, and many craft traditions that had once been passed from generation to generation gradually fell into decline. It is therefore encouraging to see how popular traditional crafts have become over the past fifteen years. Many people are keen to rediscover the crafts of their grandmothers; pastimes such as knitting and crochet are no longer viewed only as an exercise in thrift, but as a creative and rewarding activity.

This elegant cushion celebrates the best of vintage-inspired design, harking back to genteel times with its restrained colour and sophisticated surface pattern. Repeated patterns of knitted diamond shapes are enhanced by the placement of co-ordinating beads.

Size
Approximately 41cm (16½in) square

Square cushion pad,
45cm (18in) square

Materials
Rowan Cashsoft 4ply
in light green,
5 x 50g (1¾oz) balls

Debbie Abrahams beads size 6
in bronze (601),
1 x 500 bead pack

Wooden buttons,
5 x 15mm (⅝in)

3mm (US 2/3) knitting needles
Knitter's sewing or tapestry needle

Tension
27 stitches and 42 rows to 10cm (4in) square over stocking stitch when using 3mm (US 2/3) knitting needles. Adjust the needle size to achieve the correct tension.

Threading instructions

Thread beads onto yarn but remember that more than one ball of yarn is used and some balls will be used for the back of the cushion.

Front

Cast on 111 sts.

Row 1 (RS): Reading the chart from right to left, work to the repeat indicator line 11 times, then work the st beyond the repeat indicator line.

Row 2 (WS): Reading the chart from left to right, work first st of the row to the repeat indicator line, then the remainder of the row by repeating the sts between the repeat indicator line and the right of the chart 11 times, placing beads as indicated. Repeat the last 2 rows until 10 pattern repeats have been completed, ending with chart row 1 when the piece measures 41cm (16½in) from cast-on edge. Cast off.

Lower Back panel

With the right side facing, pick up and knit 111 sts along cast-off edge of Front. This will count as row 1 of the chart.

Work as for Front from row 2 until 7 pattern repeats have been completed, ending with chart row 1 when the piece measures 30cm (12in) from picked-up seam. Cast off.

Upper Back panel

With the right side facing, pick up and knit 111 sts along cast-on edge of Front.

Next row (WS): K1, *p1, k1; repeat from * to end of row.
Set moss stitch as follows:

Row 1 (RS): K1, *p1, k1; repeat from * to end of row.

Row 2 (WS): Repeat row 1.
Repeat these two rows until piece measures 13cm (5⅛in) from cast-on seam, ending with a WS row.

Next row (buttonhole cast-off row) (RS): Keeping stitch pattern correct as set work 18 sts, *cast off 3 sts, keeping stitch pattern correct as set and counting the st on the right-hand needle after the last buttonhole, work 15 sts; repeat from * to 3 sts, k1, p1, k1. (5 buttonholes)

Next row (buttonhole cast-on row): Keeping stitch pattern correct as set work 18 sts, *turn, using the cable method and wrapping the final stitch, cast on 3 sts, turn, keeping stitch pattern correct as set work 15 sts; repeat from * to 3 sts, k1, p1, k1. (111 sts)
Continue in stitch pattern as set until piece measures 17cm (7in) from cast-on seam ending with a RS row. Cast off.

Finishing

Pin out the Front and Back pieces onto a padded surface and lightly block.

Using mattress stitch, sew the side seams. Weave loose ends into the seam stitches.

Secure buttons to the Lower Back panel in line with the buttonholes.

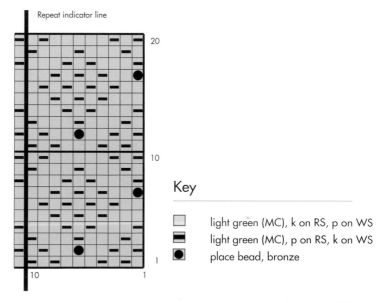

Key

▢	light green (MC), k on RS, p on WS
▬	light green (MC), p on RS, k on WS
●	place bead, bronze

Techniques Guide

The aim of this book is not to instruct you in technique but to enthuse you in your craft and inspire you with ideas for the home. All the techniques used in this book can be found in good reference books, but here is a quick reminder of some of the more unusual techniques you will use most often.

Preparation

First, it is important to always read through a pattern – not just the materials list, but the whole pattern. This will give you an idea of what is involved and where you may have to concentrate a little harder. Sometimes it is useful to photocopy a pattern and highlight special abbreviations and sections that might need more of your attention. However, don't be put off if there is something you don't understand; often it all makes sense when you have reached that point in the pattern and you have the partially worked project in front of you.

Once you have read through the pattern, work through the pattern from start to finish. Note the finished size, check you have the required materials and work a tension swatch in the yarn and needles or hook you intend using. If the tension swatch does not match that given in the book, the fabric drape will not be the same and the finished project size will not match that given at the beginning of the pattern.

Threading beads

It is essential that any beads needed for a project are threaded onto the yarn before you begin to knit or crochet. A knitter's needle or tapestry needle will be far too large to thread the beads used in this book. To thread the beads onto yarn, you will need strong sewing thread and a fine sewing needle.

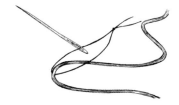

1 Thread the needle with the sewing cotton and knot the ends to form a loop. Move the knot so that it is not in line horizontally with the needle.

2 Place the end of the yarn through the loop created by the sewing thread, then pass the beads over the eye of the needle and push them down onto the sewing thread and then onto the yarn.

Knitting

The patterns in this book use basic knitting techniques to their best advantage, but there are a few you might not use on every project and for which you might find a reminder useful.

Short-row shaping

Short-row shaping is where a partial or short row is worked and the knitting is turned midway through a row to create extra rows in a certain area of a project without casting off any stitches or leaving holes. The technique used in this book involves wrapping a stitch before you turn the work and then, as directed by the pattern, picking up the wraps – working the wrapping strand together with the stitch around which it was wrapped, to prevent a hole forming in the knitted fabric. If you pick up all of the wrapped stitches using these techniques, the wraps should not be visible on the right side of the finished knitting.

In this book, short-row shaping is used in many of the circular projects where stitches are cast on for the radius of the project and more rows are worked around the outer edges of the circle than in the centre.

Wrapping a stitch on a knit row

Work as directed to the turn.

1 Slip the next stitch purlwise onto the right-hand needle.

2 Bring the yarn forward between the two needles.

3 Slip the stitch back onto the left-hand needle and take the yarn to the back. The wrap lies around the base of the slipped stitch. Turn the work and work the next row as instructed in the pattern.

Wrapping a stitch on a purl row

Work as directed to the turn.

1 Slip the next stitch purlwise onto the right-hand needle.

2 Take the yarn between the two needles to the back of the work.

3 Slip the stitch back onto the left-hand needle and bring the yarn between the two needles to the front of the work. Turn the work and work the next row as instructed in the pattern.

Picking up wraps on a knit row

Work to the first wrapped stitch.

1 Insert the right-hand needle up through the front of the wrap.

2 Then, insert the needle knitwise into the stitch it is wrapped around. Do not to do it purlwise, this will twist the stitch.

Picking up wraps on a purl row

Work to the first wrapped stitch.

1 Using the right-hand needle, pick up the wrap from the back to the front and slip the loop onto the left-hand needle.

2 Purl the loop together with the stitch it is wrapped around.

Tucks

Tucks are folds of fabric that form ridges in the fabric. They can be worked on knit or purl rows and can be of any depth. Work as directed in the pattern.

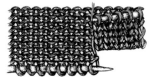

1 Mark the first row of the tuck. Work st st for twice the required depth of the tuck. Fold the tuck fabric in half, wrong sides facing. Insert the tip of the left-hand needle into the lower loop of the first stitch on the first row of the tuck from back to front.

2 Place the loop onto the left-hand needle and work the loop together with the next stitch on the left-hand needle. Continue across the row, working the corresponding stitches and loops together.

Slip stitch beading

This popular beading technique allows beads to be placed on every alternate stitch and row.

Placing beads on a right-side row – between two knit stitches

Beads are placed with the right side facing; the beads will appear on the right side.

1 Work to the position of the bead, ensuring the yarn is at the front of the work, and slide a bead down the yarn to the base of the needle. Slip the next stitch purlwise.

2 Take the yarn to the position required for the next stitch, making sure the bead stays in front of the slipped stitch. Work the next stitch quite tightly.

Placing beads on a wrong-side row – between two purl stitches

Beads can be placed on a wrong-side row so that the beads appear on the right side of the fabric. Take the yarn between the two needles to the back of the work, slide the bead down the yarn to the base of the needle, slip the next stitch knitwise, then take the yarn to the front again.

Intarsia

This technique links blocks of colour – each block with its own length of yarn. It is important you use this technique when directed as the materials recommendation is based on the single-thickness fabric this technique produces.

To link the blocks, lay the old colour over the new colour, drop the old colour, pick up the new colour and, with the yarn from the old colour looped over the new colour, work the next stitch. Continue linking the blocks at each colour change until the row is completed.

Stranded knitting

Sometimes described as Fair Isle; stranding produces a thicker fabric than the intarsia technique, as strands of unworked yarn span the reverse of the worked stitches.

Try thinking of stranded knitting as a series of stitches where each yarn is used as required and the other yarn awaits its turn. There are some simple tricks for achieving a smooth fabric. For instance, try using a knitting needle a size larger than you would use for stocking stitch. Also try using straight knitting needles or circulars with a long solid needle section; this allows you to arrange the stitches evenly along the solid section before each colour change so the strand behind the worked stitches is just the right length.

Buttonholes

The buttonholes in this book are worked over two rows. The first row is the 'cast off' row and the next row is the 'cast on' row. The buttonhole positions for the recommended button size have been worked out for you.

Cast off row (right side facing)

Work the stitches to the first buttonhole as directed in the pattern. To start the casting off process, you will need to work two more stitches before you pass one stitch over the top of another and cast off one stitch. Then cast off the required number of stitches. You will be left with one stitch on your right knitting needle to the left of the cast-off stitches. This stitch counts as the first stitch in the block of stitches between buttonholes.

Cast on row (wrong side facing)

Work the stitches to the first buttonhole as directed in the pattern. Use the cable method to cast on all but one of the required number of stitches. Then insert the needle between the first two stitches on the left needle and make a new stitch using the cable method. Before you transfer this stitch to the left needle, bring the yarn forward between the two needles (as if to purl), then place the final cast-on stitch on to the left needle in the usual way.

Wrapping the last stitch keeps the hole nice and tight and means you don't get a 'baggy' buttonhole.

Crochet

The patterns in this book do not reinvent crochet techniques but hopefully reinvent how you look at them. A knitter with a basic knowledge of crochet should find projects achievable.

Double crochet beading

This beading technique allows beads to be placed on every stitch and row. Beads are placed with the wrong side facing, but the beads will appear on the right side.

1 Work to where a bead is required. Slide the bead along the yarn so that it sits against the right side of the fabric. Insert your hook through the next stitch.

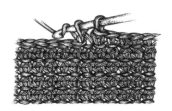

2 Wrap the yarn around the hook and bring it through the stitch. Wrap the yarn around the hook and complete the stitch, holding the bead in place.

Cross stitch

Using cross stitch on a background of tight double crochet can be a very effective way of adding adornment to a crochet piece.

On a graph, the cross stitch occupies the space of one or a multiple of squares on the grid; these are usually indicated by either a block of colour or a symbol of some kind.

With the right side facing, bring the needle through from the back and make a diagonal stitch to the upper left corner of the crochet stitch. Bring the needle through the work from back to front at the base of the left side of the crochet stitch. Pass over the first part of the stitch to the upper right corner of the crochet stitch. Insert the needle from front to back through the work to complete the stitch.

Finishing

It is not all over when the knitting and crochet is completed. This is when the true crafter gets really stuck in. If you think about it for just a moment, your work has been pulled in and out of bags, provided solace when you were in a contemplative mood, and calmed you when you were excited. Now, to look its best, your knitted or crocheted fabric needs some care and attention.

Blocking

Blocking or pressing a fabric is a technique used to set a shape before seaming or before a project is ready for display. The careful blocking of edges will also make the edges easier to stitch.

Dampen the fabric carefully, without stretching and pulling it. If you do not have the time to wash your work, spray it gently with clean water. Pin out the work, face down, using large-headed pins, and then spray with water or set with steam. If the correct tension was achieved and maintained, the project measurements given should be an accurate guide to the size of the piece.

If you do choose to lightly press the work, gently ease the fabric into shape, then, taking care that the hot baseplate of the iron does not touch your work, use the steam setting to set the shape. If you allow the iron baseplate to touch any glass beads they may shatter and so may your dreams for the project! Leave the work to dry away from direct sunlight or a heat source and turn it occasionally.

Grafting

In this book, waste yarn is used to make the process easier. Place the knit pieces flat with the right sides facing, one edge above the other. Thread a tapestry needle with a length of yarn.

1 On the lower piece of fabric, from the back, bring the needle up through the centre of the first stitch below the waste yarn, on the right of the fabric.

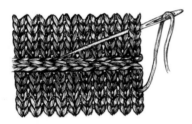

2 On the upper piece of fabric, pass the needle under both loops of the corresponding stitch.

3 On the lower piece of fabric, insert the needle through the centre of the stitch where the yarn last emerged on that piece and up through the centre of the next stitch to the left. On the upper piece of fabric, pass the needle under both loops of the corresponding stitch. Make sure that the sewn stitches are the same tension as the knitted stitches. Continue until the seam has been stitched. Unpick the waste yarn.

Mattress stitch on a knit fabric

Place the knit pieces flat with the right sides facing. Thread a tapestry needle with a length of yarn.

1 To start, draw a figure-of-eight path with the yarn and needle. On the right-hand piece, insert the needle from the back through the centre of the first stitch of the first row. Repeat on the left-hand piece and then through the same stitch on the right-hand piece and the same stitch on the left-hand piece.

2 On the right-hand piece, insert the needle from the front, through the middle of the stitch where the yarn last emerged from on that side and under the bar of yarn that divides that stitch from the one above.

3 Repeat on the left-hand piece. Continue in a zigzag fashion until the seam has been stitched.

Mattress stitch on a crochet fabric

Place the crochet pieces flat with the right sides facing. Thread a tapestry needle with a length of yarn.

On the left-hand piece, working one stitch in from the edge, insert the needle through the work from front to back one row up from the lower end and to the front of the work one stitch up. On the right-hand piece, insert the needle into the corresponding stitch from front to back and to the front of the work one stitch up. On the left-hand piece, insert the needle into the stitch where the yarn last emerged on that piece and to the front one stitch up. Repeat on the right-hand piece. Continue in this way until the whole seam has been stitched.

Double crochet seam

Hold the two crochet pieces together with right sides facing inwards. Place your left index finger between the two pieces to open the seam.

Insert the hook through a stitch on the front piece and the corresponding stitch on the back piece. Wrap the yarn around the hook and work a double crochet stitch.

Dorset buttons

These traditional buttons are made using curtain rings. They can be created in almost endless permutations of colour and are quick to make.

Using a long end of yarn, cover a curtain ring with blanket stitch. Sew over both the ring and the yarn tail until it is hidden.

Using a contrasting yarn, wrap across the ring to create the spokes of a web. Secure the centre of the spokes with a few stitches.

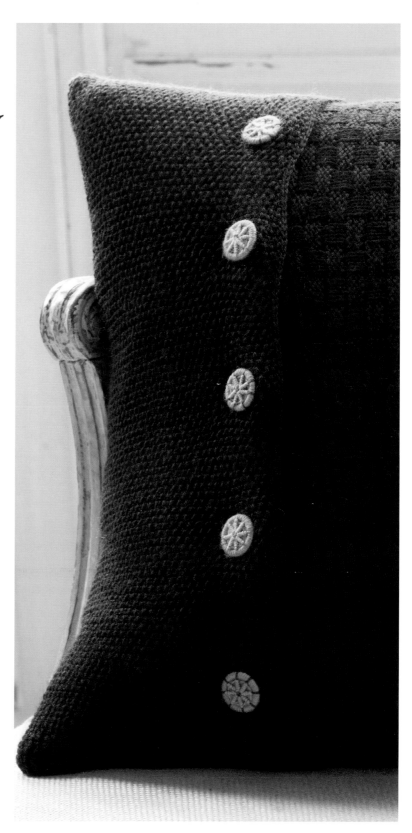

Using a third yarn colour, thread the needle through from the back to the front of the button, close to the centre of the spokes. Fill in the centre of the ring by working backstitch around the spokes of the web. Fasten off the yarn.

Abbreviations

alt	alternate
approx	approximately
beg	beginning
C6B	cable six back
C6F	cable six front
CC	contrast colour
ch-sp	chain space
ch(s)	chain(s)
CL	cluster
cm	centimetre
cont	continue
dc	double crochet
dec	decrease
dk	double knitting
dtr	double treble crochet
foll(s)	following
g	grams
gr	group
in	inches
inc	increase
k	knit
k2tog	knit two stitches together
m1	make 1
MB	make bobble
MC	main colour
oz	ounces
p	purl
p2tog	purl two stitches together
patt	pattern
pb	place bead
psso	pass the slip stitch over
rem	remaining
rep	repeat
RS	right side
sl	slip
ss	slip stitch
st(s)	stitch(es)
st st	stocking stitch
tbl	through the back of the loop
tch	turning chain
tog	together
tr	treble crochet

WS	wrong side
yo	yarn over
yrh	yarn round hook
[]	work the directions within the square bracket as directed
*	work instructions after the * as directed

Crochet Terms

UK	US
Double crochet (dc)	Single crochet (sc)
Treble crochet (tr)	Double crochet (dc)
Half treble crochet (htr)	Half double crochet (hdc)
Double treble crochet (dtr)	Treble or triple crochet (tr)
Slip stitch (ss)	Slip stitch (ss)

Yarn Information

Yarn ranges and shades are continuously reviewed and updated depending upon sales and current fashions. Designing a collection can take a long time, and yarn availability also varies depending upon global location. We felt it would be helpful to give you a list of yarn specifications so that you can find the nearest match.

Rowan Cashsoft 4ply
Superfine (fingering); US yarn weight system #1; 28sts/10cm (4in). Fibre: 57% extra fine Merino wool; 33% acrylic microfibre; 10% cashmere. 160m (175yds)/ 50g (1¾oz) ball.

Rowan Siena 4ply
Superfine (fingering); US yarn weight system #1; 28sts/10cm (4in). Fibre:100% mercerised cotton.140m (153yds)/ 50g (1¾oz) ball.

Amy Butler Belle Organic DK
Light (DK); US yarn weight system #3; rec. 22–24 sts to 10cm (4in). Fibre: 50% organic cotton; 50% organic wool. 120m (131yds)/50g (1¾oz) ball.

Rowan Cotton Glace
Light (DK); US yarn weight system #3; 23sts/10cm (4in). Fibre: 100% cotton. 115m 126yds)/ 50g (1¾oz) ball.

Rowan Wool Cotton
Light (DK); US yarn weight system #3; 22–24sts/10cm (4in). Fibre: 50% Merino wool; 50% cotton. 113m (123yds)/50g (1¾oz) ball.

Rowan Revive
Light (DK); US yarn weight system #3; 22sts/10cm (4in). Fibre: 36% recycled cotton; 36% recycled silk; 28% recycled viscose. 125m (137yds)/50g (1¾oz) ball.

Rowan Handknit Cotton
Medium (worsted); US yarn weight system #4; 20sts/10cm (4in). Fibre: 100% cotton. 85m yds (93yds)/50g (1¾oz) ball.

Rowan Pure Wool Aran
Medium (worsted); US yarn weight system #4; 18sts/10cm (4in). Fibre: 100% super wash wool. 170m (186yds)/50g (1¾oz) ball.

Rowan Felted Tweed Aran
Medium (worsted); US yarn weight system #4; 16sts/10cm (4in). Fibre: 50% Merino wool; 25% alpaca; 25% viscose.87m (95yds)/50g (1¾oz) ball.

Rowan Big Wool
Super bulky (bulky); yarn weight system #6; 7sts/10cm (4in). Fibre: 100% Merino wool. 80m (87yds) per 50g (1¾oz) ball.

Acknowledgements

A book would not be a book without an acknowledgements section at the back – indeed, a book would not exist at all without the people mentioned within the acknowledgements section at the back – so here is my vote of thanks to all the amazing people and organisations who have stood by me in the process of completing this publication.

I would like to thank the team at Anova Books, especially Katie Cowan and Amy Christian, as well as Laura Russell for her stylish page design, and Luise Roberts for her meticulous checking and editing. I would also like to thank the team at Rowan Yarns, especially Kate Buller and Sharon Brant.

Thank you to Holly Jolliffe, who manages to make all her photographs into works of art and who can get great results even on days of torrential London rain!

Huge thanks to my team of knitters and crocheters: Helen Bridgwood, Heather Esswood, Amanda Golland, Nicky Hale, Erica Pask, Sharon Tyler, Natalie Warner and Fiona Winning, all of whom managed to make my drawings and samples bloom into perfectly knitted and crocheted projects.

I would like to thank the following people for helping me to brainstorm at a time that should have been set aside for relaxation: Sue and John Culligan, Cath Cinnamon, Linda Grytten, Jenny and Kevin Hawkes, and of course Bix and Bebop.

And finally – partly because I will probably never be accepting an Oscar of any description and therefore can never make THAT speech on behalf of myself and all my co-stars – I would like to thank my family, who never waver in their support of me and all of whom I love dearly and without prejudice, although I probably don't tell them so often enough because I'm too busy knitting, crocheting, scribbling, unpicking, panicking and eating…

Whatever the craft, we have the book for you – just head straight to Collins & Brown crafty HeadQuarters!

LoveCrafts is the one-stop destination for all things crafty, with the very latest news and information about all our books and authors. And it doesn't stop there…

Enter our fabulous competitions and win great prizes
Download free patterns from our talented authors
Collect LoveCrafts loyalty points and receive special offers on all our books

Join our crafting community at LoveCrafts – we look forward to meeting you!

About the Author

Jane Crowfoot taught herself to knit after being inspired by her great-grandmother's hand-made blankets and studied textile design at Winchester School of Art. In 1996, she became a Design Consultant for Rowan Yarns and went on to work with Debbie Bliss. Jane is a leader of the recent crochet revival, which has seen knitters all over the world put down their needles and pick up a crochet hook. She is the author of *The Ultimate Crochet Bible* (9781843405634).